Also by Randal Teague

Families: Where We Each Begin

JESUS AND HIS FISHERMEN

THE UNTOLD STORY

RANDAL TEAGUE

A POST HILL PRESS BOOK
ISBN: 979-8-89565-673-0
ISBN (eBook): 979-8-89565-674-7

Jesus and His Fishermen:
The Untold Story

Cover design by Jim Villaflores

This is a work of nonfiction. All people, locations, events, and situations are portrayed to the best of the author's memory.

This book, as well as any other Post Hill Press publications, may be purchased in bulk quantities at a special discounted rate. Contact orders@posthillpress.com for more information.

Post Hill Press
New York • Nashville
posthillpress.com

Published in the United States of America
1 2 3 4 5 6 7 8 9 10

To all who channeled me to the task of this writing

I reckoned from childhood that God
had made me for some purpose,
and I spent years searching for an answer.
I think, I hope, I pray these pages capture it. —RT

Contents

Why These Words and Why Now?

There has seldom been a more important time for Christians to reclaim Jesus and his message for their selves, families, and communities. This is within a context that Christianity has never been known, or been forgotten, or been side-tracked by only nominal Christians, or wrongly known among adherents of other faiths as of now.

These pages focus on why Jesus, early in his ministry, chose the intricacies of fishing as its tactical model and fishermen as his innermost circle. Why not builders, carpenters like his father Joseph and himself? Why not farmers who plant, cultivate and harvest? We will never know with certainty, but most probably he chose fishing because proselytizing has surprisingly close parallels to fishing: intention, determination, patience, frustration, success, failure, and try again and again. A somewhat surprising pattern which emerged from that is there are more references to Jesus's ties to fishing than there is to his occupation as a carpenter. Fishing, fishermen and fish were important to him.

The first four disciples called by him to his ministry were each a fisherman, and only three of his eventual twelve, each of those three a fisherman, were brought with him to be witnesses to his momentous transfiguration only months before his crucifixion. These pages are about his and their fishing but also about the centrality of fish in his miracles of multiplying and feeding multitudes, directing the netting and other capture of fish, and more. Within that "more" is the striking similarity between fishing for fish and fishing for souls. But I don't stop there, going beyond that conclusion to discuss the important contexts surrounding the emergence of Christianity, changes in Judaism underway even before Rome's destruction of the Second Temple in the year 70 AD, and what Judaism and Christianity share, from the centrality of the Ten Commandments and a shared historical foundation prior to Jesus, to forms of congregational worship, and what they don't share, including especially in their customary manners of forgiveness.

Amid the social chaos now permeating America, Christianity appears to be losing ground to other religious faiths on one hand and the lack of faith altogether on another. Other faiths often appear to be more fervently motivated inwardly and outwardly than ours centered on Jesus. It's as if the light, the promise of Christian faith, has been hidden under a basket, a practice that Jesus eschewed.

Christianity seems to be no longer a consciously *unifying* umbrella it once was. It has been dividing and subtracting instead of adding and multiplying.

Catholic and Orthodox faiths have been divided for centuries, and Roman Catholics are divided by traditionalists and progressives with its religious orders widely arrayed.

After Protestants spent centuries dividing themselves into Lutherans, Anglicans, Episcopalians, Presbyterians, Methodists, Baptists and more, the IRS estimates there may be 30,000 tax-exempt variations in the United States alone.

Those realities noted, Protestant denominations are most recently shredding themselves by gender, equity and other divisions, self-flagellating for not having raised them centuries before, subtracting and dividing, which endangers the centrality of Jesus's message of loving one another. Many churches have taken off their roadside signage what was not long ago their denomination, maybe a good thing, maybe not.

That unifying factor of love seems to be losing to the divisiveness of what makes Christians different, rather than more or less the same, a victory of the organizational politics and the power which can come with material success instead of a recognition that, while "My kingdom is not of this world" was Jesus's own description, this world is, for each of us, the framework of life's choices.

Many once-prestigious Christian divinity schools are now seen as lack-of-divinity platforms for atheists, agnostics and downright enemies of religious faith.

Sunday schools to orient the youngest generation along a path of spiritual succession have yielded to household requirements of Sunday morning soccer or whatever other sports practice, that time of day being the only one when youngsters will agree to go for more than an hour without their cell phones.

Are these realities evidences of decline or a misunderstood opening for a broader base? The dramatic drop in regular church attendance speaks loudly of the unwillingness of individuals and families to go to a worship service in large measure echoing the political debate of the moment. "Let's go!" is losing ground each week to "Why go?"

From amidst these trends and consequences, how can Christians buttress themselves and reinforce their faith? The broadest answer is that expressions of Christianity need to regain the commanding heights of public opinion: in religious edifices, in classrooms and extracurricular settings from kindergarten through college, on news broadcasts and in entertainment venues, in law schools and courts of justice, and among associations of volunteers. Proud personal and family expressions of faith need to replace defensive cringe at their mention.

I cannot make any of that happen, but I do set out words from Jesus's own persuasive case for his role on Earth, made more understandable by their contexts, about which Christians know much but not all and, alas, often too little. Knowing more should bring back those who have given priorities to other matters in their lives and reach those that have heard too little or never heard at all. I do this by setting out a comprehensive understanding of Jesus, the first Christian century's geographic, political, cultural and religious contexts surrounding him, and the core of his messages, his persuasive teaching methods, and even his frustrations, especially his frustration with those closest to him, from his family and neighbors to even his disciples.

No matter by which translation, the books of the New Testament are about 300 pages in combined length. Within this book's cover are several hundred more pages with additional meanings of the Gospels, the acts of the apostles and what has been written about them over the course of nearly two millennia. They are an exciting addition to Judeo-Christian discussions, particularly about the first century of the Christian era. They also analogize Jesus's first-hand knowledge of fishing by his disciples to his day's and our day's bringing together of willful and faithful souls.

It does not bother me, and ought not to bother you, that there are mysteries in an understanding of faith, as it does not bother me that there are mysteries in an understanding of anything else, including science. In each, answers bring forth additional questions, which singularly and together are opportunities for further inquiry, and inquiry helps to concentrate day-to-day focuses. Worshipping in a congregation is usually a once-a-week occurrence, but wondering by one's self on the knowns and unknowns of faith can occur in any moment any day or night. They should. It's mentally healthy to not know all the answers because not knowing generates streams of thought on the essences of life and stretches its boundaries into contemplation of the afterlife.

These pages also set out the importance of Christians knowing more about the Judaism from which Jesus of Nazareth came and Jews knowing more about his Christianity, growths in knowledge netting gains for each and both. We share so much already to not welcome learning more.

Lastly, I have set out my own answers to my own questions. These pages are neither a theological treatise nor a biology primer. They are my points of view on issues currently confronting my Christian faith and its ties to Judaism. My deepest hope is that they will generate many conversations among Christians and others about those issues and about these pages. You will have questions too, some of which I did not have. In some measure, that is why what follows often has a conversational tone.

Please turn the page and continue!

CHAPTER 1

Jesus and His Fishermen

There is a far too long underrecognized intersection at which Jesus and his fishermen intersect with lives being lived today. It is what he and they knew about fishing that heavily influenced the shape of his ministry and his followers' continuation of his teachings. It's an intersection that warrants the attention of each of us, for it builds further what we need to know about him and that ministry.

How did I come ever so gradually to this focus on Jesus's significant connection to fishing? Let's start at my beginning.

Fishing is for me, among it being a sport, also a spiritual event. It has those other dimensions, but permeating them is that spirituality. Place has something to do with the bringing out of that feeling. Fishing brings me to the waters which flow over the face of our planet. In morning's first light or evening's coming darkness, I am awed at planets, stars, and even galaxies appearing as mere twinkles, and I know with confidence that I am not alone. Taken all together, these moments cause me to wonder what lies both within and beyond me.

I've been blessed in catching tarpon along Central America's Caribbean shoreline jungles and sailfish off its mountainous Pacific coast, Nile perch in East Africa's largest of lakes, tuna and dolphin in the Gulf Stream, and white salmon from the nearly frozen waters of Russian Siberia. Add the fierce vampire fish of the Orinoco River between Colombia and Venezuela, halibut off Alaska's south coast, flounder in the Atlantic's barrier island channels, trout in streams too many to count, and lowly shad in the Potomac within sight of the Kennedy Center in our nation's capital. I've also had days and nights in which I hooked not a single finny creature. It's at moments like those that I tamp down my disappointment by recalling that Jesus's disciples, future saints though they were, had frustrating days and nights of empty nets on the Sea of Galilee.

When I walk the shorelines of that iconic sea, I do so aware of the roles that fishermen and their fish had in the life of Jesus.

He chose Galilee and its inland sea around which to build his ministry.

He centered that ministry around fishing villages, especially Capernaum and Magdala.

His first four disciples were each a fisherman.

He lived most of his last years in the house of a fishing family, that being the house of Simon Peter's mother-in-law.

Three, each a fisherman, of his twelve disciples witnessed his supernatural transfiguration.

Jesus filled his disciples' nets with abundant fish when those disciples had failed to catch any or many.

He fed more than 5,000 men, plus accompanying women and children, with two fish and five loaves of bread that he miraculously multiplied, this demonstration of his God-like power set out in all four Gospels. That two and that five add to seven, the biblical number representing completion and perfection, the fish and the loaves coming from a probably not-yet-sinful boy in contrast to the lives of the multitude of adults.

He used Peter's fishing boat as a platform from which to address a multitude.

His fishermen used boats to transport him from shore to shore to avoid lengthy and treacherous overland travel.

He even identified a fish with a coin in its mouth in order to have the fish caught and the coin removed by Peter to pay a temple tax.

At his meeting with the eleven disciples after his resurrection, he inquired, "Do you have anything here to eat?" and "they gave him a piece of broiled fish, and he took it and ate it in their presence."

There is no way to confirm this, nor is there a need to do so, but Jesus may have joined his fishermen when they needed help from arms and hands as strong as his as a carpenter, a builder. There is no account of that in scripture, maybe because there was no need for it in light of his extensive relationship with Peter and his boat's crew. His help would have been that of a close friend helping a short-handed fisherman, Peter, whose family gave him the better part of three years of eating, sleeping, and talking under the same roof. From those few years emerged Christianity. The Hebrew word *mishpacha* means someone so close to a family that they are treated as one even though they are not a blood relative. That was Jesus in Peter's household.

The symbol of that faith in its first centuries was a simple two-line diagram of a fish. Further, the Greek word for fish, *ichthys*, is the Greek acronym for "Jesus Christ, God's Son, Savior."

Because different territorial authorities control the Sea of Galilee's eastern shoreline, Israeli border security has not permitted recreational fishing in it. That notwithstanding, walking along its western and northern shorelines on the Israeli side is among the highest valued of my overseas experiences. These walks are my reach back to Jesus and his disciples in the territorial space of their lives, and I hope they will be yours, for you will understand the Bible and Jesus's earthly life much more effectively if you actually walk in his footsteps in the Holy Land.

There is an important thought which arises from scripture that upon following death and upon salvation the surviving spirit will be ushered into universal knowledge. My response to that thought, that hope, is a profound "Wow!" As that knowledge will relate to Jesus, we will know:

- Where, and doing what, he spent the years between twelve and thirty, those eighteen being over half of his physical life on Earth.
- More about Mary, about whom we already know much, and about Joseph, about whom we know far less.
- The contextual and factual intentions for his innermost circle, brethren, disciples, apostles, and missionaries as their definitions matured. In doing that, he could set forth how he selected them, including, for me, whether John the Baptist advised him at least as to some of them in discussions following Jesus's baptism.
- The miracles set out and those not set out in the Gospels, especially as to the ways in which they changed the lives of those made whole.
- Why he chose Peter to be the rock on which his teachings were to be built, especially in light of Peter's lack of courage after that choosing and in contrast to the Paul-reinforced stamina which assured the completion of his and their tasks in building the faith.

- Whether he brought Paul into the leadership of the emerging faith principally because Peter needed shoring up.
- End uncertainties about Mary Magdalene.

This knowledge would add measurably to our understanding of him, them, his mission and his ministry. They would affirm two millennia of accuracies on one hand and correct misunderstandings or offset inadvertent or intended errors which followed on the other.

The answers would more accurately connect our time with theirs. They would help Christians to better understand Christianity. They would help those of other faiths to better understand Christianity. They would help us to better understand them and their faiths.

CHAPTER 2

Galilee and Its Neighbors

A person who has not been to Galilee and Judea probably has mental images of them and their ancientness. They are most often recollections from artists depictions, the kinds one finds in illustrated Bibles. Galilee itself in those years was a land of Jews and Gentiles because it was a land of centuries of outward and inward migrations.

Before the Maccabean period began a century and a half before Jesus's birth, few Jewish families lived in Galilee. Those that did had returned over a protracted captivity of Jews in Babylon. Galilee's Nazareth was a new village at the time of Jesus's birth in Bethlehem south of Judea's Jerusalem. There is little evidence of the earliest settlement from which Nazareth grew, although archaeologists continue to add to it. What evidence there is includes the ancient tombs which defined its allowable boundaries. Galilee's dominance by Gentiles declined after its conquest by the Maccabean leader John Hyrcanus and his sons, for they were determined to populate it with returning Jews. They gave its predominant Greek and other Gentile populations a choice between accepting Judaism by circumcision or leaving. Some converted, some who did not convert departed, and others must have managed to remain, for the Greek population was flourishing in the region by the time of Jesus.

Galilee remained a frontier region not just occupied by but also surrounded by those different peoples, each identified by their dominant language, religion, and culture. Each people's history presaged its future, and each people's future bound up its aspirations. The Phoenician region of Sidon and Tyre was to Galilee's northwest, greater Roman Syria was to its northeast, and Roman Nabatea was to its east. In short, Galilee was hemmed in.

Even the word Galilee is a Graecized form of the Hebrew *galil*, meaning folding or rolling as are the hills north of Judea where Galilee's southern region ends. Much of Galilee consisted then and now of those hills. The name's complete root, *galil hag-goyim,* denotes a region of those hills populated by peoples other than Jews, capturing accurately this geography and history, *goyim* being Hebrew for someone not Jewish.

Albeit surrounded by and interspersed among these other peoples, Galileans developed their own identity and characteristics, described by scholar E.W.G. Masterman as independence of character, resourcefulness, and readiness to defend themselves and their land, traits which survive in the modern era. Between the bookends of ancient pasts and modern circumstances, these lands and their Jewish people suffered conquests, occupations and expulsions, followed by returns and restorations. The in-migrations after World Wars I and II were simply its most recent returns.

In global geographic contexts, Galilee is that part of western Asia which we know as the Middle East, albeit not in the East's middle but rather a proximate midpoint between Europe to the west and Asia to the east. We also know this region as Asia Minor and as the Levant, French for "the east" as the horizon from which the sun rises. Galilee's western boundary is the Mediterranean Sea where Joppa, now a neighborhood in Tel Aviv, and Caesarea were its principal ports, and where Haifa to its north is now its largest. To its immediate south were mountainous Samaria and then Judea, the latter being the heartland of Israel and culturally distinct from Galilee and known in large measure for its dominant Jerusalem. Upper Galilee is so named for it is both north and coincidentally higher in altitude. Lower Galilee is so named for it is south and descends below the Mediterranean's sea level to its Sea of Galilee and it in turn to the Dead Sea, the world's lowest and largest lake below sea level.

Galilean history stretches back thousands of years and is tied significantly to that Hebrew nation known now as ancient Israel. Israel's modernity is anchored in its long past, whose nineteenth and twentieth centuries witnessed the struggle for Jews to return to their originating lands. Jewish and Israeli tied histories gave birth to Galilee's and Israel's determinations not to be overrun by hostile forces of which there were many. This concern preceded its hostile occupation by Rome following hospitable Greece's.

By the time of Jesus, Galilee had been settled with scattered communities for at least 7,000 years, though nothing about them was recorded in writing until an account of Egyptian Pharaoh Thutmose III's victory over the Canaanites at his Battle of Megiddo. Beyond writings, the earliest known inscription of the word "Israel" is found on a thirteenth-century BC Merneptah Stele discovered in Egypt. Its pre-history is known from archaeological evidence of communities and religious sites, household and hunting stone and bone tools, extensive potteries, woven and sewn fabrics, carved figurines, and cave art from combinations of ochres, minerals, burned bone meal and charcoal mixed in water, animal fats, tree saps, and even blood. Those activities led to communities and their presumably well-considered decisions to have governance. The ancient site of Tel Megiddo, "tel" meaning "mound," as in an appreciable hill, as in modern Tel Aviv, overlooks a valley known by its Greek name as Armageddon, made widely known by James Michener's *The Source.* Tel Megiddo is now a World Heritage Site containing twenty-six layers of ruins reaching back to the Neolithic Age. It guarded an important section of the Via Maris trade route from the far and near east to the Mediterranean to its west. The successes and failures of competing peoples caused boundaries to be redrawn many times and their place names to be changed.

The hundred years surrounding Jesus's birth were not only a period of increased Roman domination of Galilee but also of its domination of southern Europe, northern Africa, and the greater Near East. By its end, Rome had conquered ancient Israel and pushed further east, conquered Britain to its west, while pushing farther north into Germanic lands. Galilee gained attention in Rome from being within the empire's quarter of the known world's estimated population, albeit a time of extraordinary changes in and out of Rome and of a 200-year sequence of Jewish rebellions. Caesar Augustus rose to power, ruled, died, and was followed by others, a Caesar's authority and its exercise counterpoised in a seesaw manner with the Roman Senate's growing and ebbing authorities.

Lower Galilee became particularly important in Jesus's ministry, and the combination of its geographic centrality and its porous borders served the medium to amplify his teachings and other peoples' knowledge of his ministry. Masterman captured that in these words in 1909, four decades before modern Israel gave rise to today's stark and often hostile realities:

> While nature provided Jesus with such abundant illustrations, the climate made possible a mode of life for his ministry only practicable in such a land. Days of unbroken sunshine and nights of pleasant warmth can be counted for six or seven months every year; it is possible, without fear of rain, to gather crowds on the hill sides day and night all over the district. The moonlight nights are perfect for rest out of doors; or, if the days are oppressively hot, for travel. Never was a land more suited for itinerant work and open-air preaching. Even in midwinter it is no uncommon thing to have six weeks of sunshine without shower. The conditions of peasant life in the east, though hard in some ways, leave much spare time, especially between sowing and harvest, for leisure and thought; food is cheap and wants are few; what is not done today can often be equally well done tomorrow.

In large measure, these idyllic conditions have given way to the consequences of the modern age's communications, transportation, other technologies, migrations, and hostile neighbors.

Some of the typography of ancient and modern Israel is that of "a dry and barren land," but that image can be misleading. Areas in Lower Galilee are green and lush in springtime. Upper Galilee to its north and Judea to its south, too, are green and brown, in places lands of blanketing vegetation and in others of stone, gravel and sand. Galilean landscapes include cliff and hillside patterns of massive fallen stones from eons of weather and earthquakes. It is a land of strikingly beautiful botanical landscapes, especially as wildflowers' roots watered by winter rains push forth spring blossoms by the millions. The fragrances of honeysuckle and jasmine are carried by the breezes which come from the Mediterranean down through its valleys. Early spring times were then and are now comfortable for walking on trails through these blossoms and stones. Such a walk then would have been a momentary escape from other realities of life.

Galilee lies where the temperate and semitropical zones meet, fertile lands east and west of the lake with deserts and mountains surrounding them. This assures weather from winter's cold to summer's sweltering heat, but it is not the season alone which produces these variations. Location, especially altitude, can change from winter-like to summer-like temperatures in less than twenty miles. In their and our times winters stretch over days and nights which can be quite pleasant and others that can be surprisingly harsh.

The Sea of Galilee's winter temperatures run in the mid-50°s F. I have been in Jerusalem with snow under foot, but there was more snow, as there often is, at the higher borders with Lebanon and Syria. I have been only sixty miles east in Amman, Jordan, with more than half a foot of snow on the airport tarmac, but snows melt quickly in this region. Summer temperatures in Lower Galilee easily exceed 100° F with the highest that I recall from weather records of the northern Jordan Valley at 129°F. There is nothing but hot air on such a day and its night with temperatures that burn your throat as you talk or labor at breathing. Those temperatures drive the lake's water from cool to warm to downright unwelcoming.

Jesus's fishermen avoided oppressive daytime heat by fishing at night and by occasionally pouring wooden buckets of water over themselves and the minimal clothing in which they sweltered. We know from scripture that Peter sometimes fished while naked, whatever definition captured that description, and he would not have been alone in that respect. Historical accounts attest to weather so hot that persons ashore tried to sleep partially submerged in water. Lest it be overlooked, there was also a commercial reason why Jesus's fishermen plied their skills at night. Those at docks who sized, acquired, gutted, and further processed fish for markets did so in the somewhat lesser heat of the morning, which meant that freshly caught fish had to be at the shoreline before or soon after sunrise.

To Galilee's immediate south and tightly tied to its ancientness was Judea, the place name for the land of Judah, a territory of geographic, military, and political significance occupied by Israelite tribes and their later kingdom. As a hilly part of ancient Palestine's West Bank, Judea's capture, together with Samaria, by Israel in 1967 resulted in the area's present name of Yehuda. To Jerusalem's east was Jericho and beyond that the former Ottoman province and later British protectorate of Transjordan, mostly now the kingdom of Jordan.

Galilean and Judean borders changed little over time, but their successive foreign occupations had different characteristics, especially as to the extents of ranges of oppressions. The life of Jesus was a timeframe within the Romans' disregard of the primarily local religion of Judaism and their disrespectful tolerance of its high priests and semi-sovereigns. A significant consequence of their occupation was the transfer of government authority from once-independent Jewish rulers to Jewish officials exercising only delegated authority from Rome. Phrased another way, they did what Roman leaders required of them, and one of those leaders stands out in Christian history. Appointed the fifth Roman Prefect of Judea, as well as Idumea to its south and Samaria to its north and during the rule of the emperor Tiberius, Pontius Pilate was the procurator, that's the governor, of only a single, albeit important, territory within Rome's larger Syrian province. There were reasons and emotions in his political calculations in Rome which were transferred in his thinking to the similar hierarchal contexts of the Jerusalem under his jurisdictional and anatomical feet. Hostile emotions he did have, for the Romanized Jewish historian Josephus's and Hellenistic Jewish philosopher Philo's writings refer to his conduct as arrogant, abusive, venal, violent, even savage, and his official acts as including violation of Jews' holy places and the near total theft of the sacred Temple's treasury. The powers in Rome may have concluded he was exactly the type of ruler necessary to govern this land of violent upheavals and self-described stiff-necked locals. In that Pilate served in this post from 26 BC to 36 or 37 AD, his encounter with Jesus occurred during his mid years. We shall return to him at Jesus's trials and crucifixion.

Winter rains in the region were and remain important to agriculture, husbandry, and fisheries. Before the modern age's linguistic differentiations, the Arabic word for rain was synonymous with winter, for they were conjoined in the mind's reflections on seasonal weather. As to the physical features of Galilee, one of major importance is its large number of alluvial plains and their rich soil for the growth of crops for harvest and flowers for beauty's sake. As to the flowers brought forth by these rains, yellow chrysanthemums, white narcissuses, red anemones and ranunculus, pink, white, and purple cyclamen, hibiscus, Nazareth irises, purple lupinus, rose-colored mallows, red tulips, white umbels, and other flowers grow abundantly in Galilean spring times. Israel has 2,500 other species, many of them in Galilee, so there is no shortage of seasonal colors in its meadows and on its hillsides. The lilies of Galilee's fields caused Jesus to observe their beauty as surpassing Solomon in all their splendor. Taken from vantage points primarily at its north and northwest, vistas eastward and southward can be awesome for they are mostly devoid of modern construction.

These rains contribute to root pressure for a new cycle of growth within its fruit and other trees. Fruits now are borne from apple, apricot, cherry, fig of several varieties (including cactus fig), kumquat, lemon, lychee, black mulberry, olive, orange, pear, persimmon, pomegranate, and tangerine trees and in certain locations date palms. Blackberry bushes abound. Almond trees and walnut trees are prevalent, and ancient pistachio trees in Upper Galilee attest to their long presence. Fruit and nut trees are not the sole repertoire of growth, for Egyptian maize, fennel, mustard, and thistle grow to the height of men, and lentils, cucumbers, pumpkins, and melons grow at their feet. Requiring water throughout their brief cycles, bananas are found in abundance where water is plentiful, quite productively about eighty miles south in the area of Jericho's springs. Wheat is grown for its flour for breads, and barley is grown for bread as well as cattle fodder. Galilee is a region of ancient trees, and black mulberry, oak, olive, Atlantic pistachio, and Syrian sniper are among them. We will explore in greater depth which woods were used in the construction of ancient Galilee's fishing boats, the species for one boat of particularly historic note being Aleppo pine, Atlantic terebinth, carob, hawthorn, laurel, plane, redbud, sidder, sycamore, and willow and cedar, the latter from Upper Galilee into Lebanon.

Who ruled these lands must be noted for the answers are profoundly relevant to Jesus and his time: Herod the Great and his four-generation family but in servitude to Roman authority. Despite the outward trappings of an autonomous monarch, Herod the Great was a vassal king in allegiance to Rome and even one with marginal Jewish identity. The historical identifier "the Great" came not from widespread appreciation of him and his rule but from his undertaking of the construction of massive building projects, most notably but not exclusively the reconstruction of the Temple and the port of Caesarea Maritima on the Mediterranean. He was named king of Judea by the Roman Senate in 40 BC, most certainly to assist Rome in assimilating the region into the empire. Thus, the title king was not given by the Jewish nation or their leaders, one argument among many for at least emotional resistance to him and his rule. He returned empowered by an army of Rome's choosing and command, not his, one which promptly defeated but did not annihilate the Parthians or their five-century empire in southwest Asia and their allied Hasmoneans. As an historical note, the three magi who brought gifts to the infant Jesus may have been Parthians, descendants from Cyrus the Great's Aramaic-speaking Achaemenid empire, the diplomatic stature of which would have gained them an audience at Herod's court. Furthermore, their mission in search of a new king in his land aroused Herod's deepest suspicions. Herod did not provoke them because they were an embassy in the original use of that diplomatic term and, as such, had to be accorded safe passage and, further and principally, he wanted them to find this new king so he could remove the threat to his rule by killing him. The later Great Jewish Revolt would begin in 66 AD, three decades after Jesus's crucifixion, and become ancient Rome's longest rebellion against it at nearly 200 years.

Herod knew well the realities of his position, living under ever-present pressure to pay heavy tribute to Rome in exchange for both his authority and the tasks of massive revenue collections to cover the costs of the government he directed and the officials and forces which Rome deployed to protect their joint and several interests. Aside from that burden, he and his family incurred sizeable expenses for the constructions of Sepphoris (Zippori) in Galilee, the Mediterranean port of Caesarea, the Tomb of the Patriarchs in Hebron, and the acropolis of Herodian in the Judean desert, as well as the reconstruction of the Temple in Jerusalem and the costs of the exorbitant lifestyle he required for himself, his family and their entourages. That's three—Roman, Judean, and Galilean—layers of government, including his own tax and related economic burdens upon his subjects. There was great contempt among many, probably most, Jews toward him.

While Herod had been raised as a Jew, he was not regarded by all among the Temple powerful to be of sufficient Jewish origin, his ancestors having been Edomites from an area roughly in today's Negev Desert and southern Jordan. The Edomites were a historic desert people converted or perhaps reconverted to Judaism during the Hasmonean period of the second and first centuries BC. Judaism emerged as a monotheistic religion from among Bronze Age polytheistic Semitic religions, by Judaism's own calculations fifty-eight centuries ago.

The most profound early consequence was Moses's forty days and forty nights encounter on the mountain top and his return's pronouncement of commandments as the fundamental basis for living the Jewish life obediently for the benefit of self and others. It was a covenant binding Jew and God together with God's love for his chosen people expressed through the requirement of their obedience to his commandments. Millennia later, there was deep resentment among observant Jews of Herod's decadent lifestyle in respect to those commandments, but he devised a political remedy to ameliorate it. He undertook the massively expensive construction of the Second Temple, enabling him to be more widely accepted by the Jewish hierarchy.

Destroyed by the neo-Babylonian king Nebuchadnezzar in 586 BC, the temple prior to the Second had been rebuilt seventy years later at the encouragement and with the support of King Cyrus II. This was Cyrus the Great who freed Hebrew slaves, permitted them to return to from where their ancestors had come, and granted religious freedom to peoples throughout his realm. They were actions of such importance that the prophet Isaiah (meaning "Yahweh is salvation") at Isaiah 45 referred to Cyrus as a messiah, the only non-Jewish person in the Hebrew Bible to be referred to as one. Isaiah 45 is a remarkable reading for, among other declarations, Isaiah makes clear that it was God who gave the non-Jewish Cyrus great powers on Earth against his enemies, and in return Cyrus treated Jews and others respectfully, including their right to worship their own god.

Herod the Great had been dead for at least twenty years by the time of the completion of the Second Temple during the rule of his great-grandson Herod Agrippa II, known to Jerusalem's occupiers as the Romanized Marcus Julius Agrippa, he being the last ruler of the Herodian dynasty. Two millennia later, the Temple's surviving Western Wall is the most significant reverential site in Judaism.

Galileans and Judeans bore the onerous burden of payments to support Herod's multitiered control of their lives, and their impoverishment was a consequence. The Herods, those who preceded them and those who succeeded them were at the top of complex systems of economic relationships, including the holding of monopolies over land and water resources, and fish did not escape their reach. They sat atop the pinnacle of a structural pyramid of taxation in its direct and indirect forms, enforcing assessments through chief tax collectors who purchased rights at auctions to harvest fish and administered them through subordinate tax collectors. Each level in this pyramid had to raise revenue sufficient to pay all amounts due to the level above them as well as secure an excess sufficient to offset their costs and thereby assure their own livelihood. This auction bid up prices at their outset and forced successively steeper collections at each time a fish moved from lake to table, altogether to such an extent that tax levels hitting fisherman and their catches were 25 percent to 40 percent, some estimate 50 percent. Some believe that Matthew's job as a tax collector in Capernaum gave him personal insights into the extent of this economic oppression of fishermen, whose number included Peter, Andrew, James, John, and others known to him, typically in stressful situations. Matthew gained much knowledge from having stood on one side, and then the other, of this multilayered taxing of fish.

To make this specific as to fish, fishing and their marketing, a fish caught in the Sea of Galilee during Jesus's time was taxed at every step of its movement from lake to plate. Whomever centuries later wrote that taxes are a form of food for politicians almost certainly did not know how accurate that observation was in relation to fish in ancient Israel. A fee had to be paid for the right to fish, a right which could be resold. As fish caught were brought ashore and counted, they were taxed. If they were salted for export, the salt was taxed and a tax on its export further added. If a fish was moved across the Galilean–Judean provincial border on its way to tables in Jerusalem and elsewhere, it was subjected to a duty for crossing that border. We know from scriptural accounts of the difficulties of fishing, but economic burdens beyond poor catches are not set out in them, but they did not disappear when the Roman Empire did. They continued through the long Ottoman period into the beginning of the twentieth century. The basic tax was set at one of each five fish, thus a 20 percent levy. However, documented and enforced, it was paid in advance in the currency of the realm every three years not to, but rather by, the tax collector (*ashshar*) to the government. That tax collector in turn retained or sold rights in whole or in part, intending to enlarge their accumulated value to him, the rise in end cost being inescapable.

Fishing was not the only over-taxed occupation. The productivity of Galilean farmland worked against its owners, because income generated by that productivity gave rise to desires among the wealthy to own their lands. Payments against mortgage debts and taxes were so onerous they could stretch over forty to fifty harvests. No wonder scholars have referred to this burden as a crushing tax yoke, the burden of taxes being one of the principal reasons for Galilean unrest generally and revolts against Roman authority specifically. Economic historians believe the de facto interest rates paid on borrowed funds reached at least 50 percent.

Ancestral family plots had to be sold to larger landowners and temple priests, or were confiscated by Herod's officials in satisfaction of unpaid debts accumulated to unpayable levels. A significant consequence was the downward transition of an entire class from land-owning farmers to servile peasants. Great economic gain came to Herod and his allies from the export of production to buyers throughout the Roman Empire, so great a gain that it was the primary reason why he ordered the building of the urgently needed Mediterranean port of Caesarea. Into these economic burdens, Joseph, Jesus, and other tradesmen, fishermen, and farmers were born, raised, worked, lived, and paid from their hard-earned incomes for the extravagances of Roman and Herodian governments.

CHAPTER 3

Galilee and the Gospels

Galilee is the principal, though not exclusive, geographic focus for what the Gospels of Matthew, Mark, and Luke set forth in their recitals of Jesus's teachings and miraculous healings. John affirms them but then moves beyond the others through a combined appeal of reason, heart, and conscience, together a recitation of the permanent things revealed by and through Jesus. John is also, more than theirs, about Jesus's presence, preaching and miracles in and near to Jerusalem in that it accounts for Jesus there at Passover in each year of his ministry: first at its beginning, second after feeding the Galilean crowds before leaving for it, and third when he returns to it for what would become his entry, trials, crucifixion, and resurrection. The Gospels are disputed by some scholars but they were each written in the contexts of personal observation, awareness, reflection and faith in Jesus. They are the four-cornered foundation of the New Testament canon as well as the predicate to the books that follow in the New Testament, which add the earliest years and events after Jesus was no longer physically present.

The dates during which the Gospels were written are debatable but the most important consideration is what they tell. Because of their order—Matthew, Mark, Luke, and John—readers may assume they were written in that order, but they were not. Mark was the first written, and his fuller account is replete with circumstances and events as they related to Jesus's life, a consequence of which is Matthew's and Luke's reliance on Mark's narrative for its details. John added more and captured Jesus more contextually and more spiritually.

While there is no unanimity among scholars as to which John wrote the Gospel of John, the preponderance of evidence is that it was the John within Jesus's innermost circle. Its details and insight had to come from someone in Jesus's presence throughout his ministry; this John is also referred to as John the Beloved and John the Blessed. He was one of the first four called by Jesus and was with him at his many signs (*semeia*) as well as the startling drama of his transfiguration, in the fabled Upper Room, in the courtyard of the high priest during the Jewish trial, in the Garden of Gethsemane the night before, and at his crucifixion. He was the first of the twelve disciples to arrive at the empty tomb and the first to later recognize the resurrected Jesus while he and other disciples were fishing off the shore of Galilee. This John is believed by many scholars to have been the only one of the twelve disciples to not be killed for their teachings and to have lived a long life, some say at modern Greece's Aegean Island of Patmos, on which John had the vision set out as the book of Revelation.

John earlier recognized the profoundest message set out through the Jesus who spoke, acted, died, and rose from death, a human embodiment of God's attributes and timeliness. Professor of biblical theology Andreas Kostenberger has reflected quite visually on another scholar's conclusion on the value of that perception: John's Gospel "is deep enough for an elephant to swim in and shallow enough for a child not to drown." I surmise that means the veracity of his setting out the authenticity of Jesus is made through layers of readers' understandings. To me, his Gospel ties Jesus, and does so profoundly, to the cosmos in ways the preceding Gospels do not as fully, and his first chapter does it in summary. On about the twentieth reading, one senses that just maybe Jesus was his ghostwriter in whatever way that could have happened.

Mark and John set out another key to understanding Jesus's earthly role, that he changed his point of view on the multitudes gathered to see and hear him, Jesus referring to them as flocks, expanding from solely Jewish gatherings to Jews and Gentiles, and sharing the importance of this broadening with his disciples so they could focus and work accordingly. Luke had the benefit of having later traveled on missionary journeys with Paul, their interactions further informing Luke's account from Paul's successful intent to expand the faith community founded by Jesus beyond its geographical origins in Galilee and Judea.

Why then was Matthew placed first among the Gospels, making it first in a testimony of the emerging and sustained new faith? There were multiple reasons: its detailed ancestry of Jesus, its heightened drama of Jesus's life and words, including vivid descriptions of his miracles, and accounts of the earliest Christian formation by its setting out of instructions which were given to emerging local faith communities. The ancestry has been disputed, a matter of significant disagreement among scholars, but I have been informed quite recently that a work is nearing completion which will confirm its accuracy. We know few details of Matthew's life, but we do know from scripture (Luke 5:27–32) that he had been a tax collector, one named Levi, for the deeply resented Roman occupiers before his call by Jesus.

By the nature of his work, a tax collector existed at the center of networks of persons and their tax-generating activities, giving him deep knowledge of their lives. This included especially those seeking to avoid payment of taxes from sources known and concealed but reluctantly paid when there was no other choice than confiscation of property, imprisonment, or worse. In Matthew's jurisdictional reach, these exigencies would have reached Capernaum's fishermen. Existing as Matthew did between Jewish taxpayers and Roman tax consumers, he would have been avoided, feared, and almost certainly hated, by taxpayers but depended on by the Romans as a source of a constant flow of information important to them.

A tax collector's value to Rome and to himself, for his own income was derived from his tax collections, depended on the breadth and depth of his knowledge and his careful attention to detail, facilitated by notetaking in at least Latin and Hebrew, and by numbers added, subtracted, divided, and multiplied. This was a skill set of later value to Jesus in an entourage of at least thirteen men and others in nearly constant movement. Matthew's knowledge of Hebrew scripture and Jesus's teaching added to the length of his Gospel narrative. It probably was important to Matthew, in contemplation of his life, that Jesus forgave persons for their sins. Matthew's financial resources would have been helpful to Jesus's mission, but it is probable that he lost all or most of it in Roman authorities' retribution for having left their employ. Because he worked with monies, it would have been logical for Matthew to be the keeper of the purse for Jesus's needs of it in support of his ministry, but he was not. That role was Judas Escariot's.

In the literary age, Mark would be praised by writers, editors, publishers, and readers as a superb storyteller. His words created the mental images a reader needed to recall them. He connected what would become a New Testament to what had preceded Jesus in Hebrew scripture, upon which the Gospel of Matthew relied more than any other Gospel. He wrote primarily for Christians emerging from Judaism, whereas Luke wrote primarily for Gentiles coming to Jesus's messages. John had "a trained mind and wrote good Greek" and in the continued words of English church historian Owen Chadwick "wrote a gospel full of insight, feeling and beauty." Chadwick is known for his conclusion set out as the opening sentence of his *A History of Christianity*, "All religion is the yearning of humanity for what lasts," a permanence captured by John.

Here is the profound John 1:1:

> In the beginning was the Word, and the Word was with God, and the Word was God. He was with God in the beginning. Through him all things were made; without him nothing was made that has been made. In him was life, and that life was the light of all mankind. This light shines in the darkness, and the darkness has not overcome it.

The past and present verb tenses there should not be seen as excluding a future tense for John clearly sets the present between a past and a future as if to have said in translation "the darkness has not overcome it and never will."

That light is a knowledge which informs wisdom and dispels ignorance. It is the truth on which all the universe rests, from the immutable laws of physical sciences to the physical and social constructions of biological beings. This light is wisdom beyond humankind's comprehension of it, a point relevant to all, but particularly to those who deny such wisdom because they lack mental acuity or interest in discerning it, often not recognizing that their knowing atheism, unknowing agnosticism, or sheer indifference reflects on their inadequacies, not God's. John's conclusion went beyond that of Mark, Matthew, and Luke's, for while each of those three saw Jesus as the foretold messiah preceding an end of days, John saw Jesus as the earthly incarnation of a divinity who existed before, was existing then and would continue to exist. I mean no affront to a science view of human experience, for I began in the study of biology myself, and science understands much, but no science is ever final. How did Genesis, first written thousands of years ago and that after a long tradition of chant, capture accurately the progression of Earth? "And God said, 'Let there be light, and there was light'." That's the Big Bang!, and so it goes through Genesis. How did the ancients know this accuracy many thousands of years before modern science did?

The Gospels present Jesus in consistent yet differing ways, a circumstance which warrants explanation. Over the course of 2,000 years, views of Jesus, his disciples, and their four Gospels became increasingly regarded as a narrative built around a core of the historical Jesus, a "mythological construct formed in the generation subsequent to the life of Jesus by people who did not personally know Jesus and who were not eyewitnesses to the events" to erode belief in him and his acts. Yet Titus Kennedy informs us in *Unearthing the Bible* that "archaeological data, and in particular many artifacts, demonstrate the accuracy and historical reliability of the Gospel narratives," the discovery of early manuscripts of the Gospels confirming the early composition of those accounts from eyewitness testimony. They establish the miracles as occurring because of divine powers expressed through the mind, words, hands, and even the garment hem of Jesus. They followed in time one commentator's conclusion that fifty-six miracles occurred in the Jews' Hebrew Bible and its Christian's Old Testament version, "miracle" defined as "God's way of showing He is God with the power to impact human events."

Jesus did not perform all his miracles in Galilee, but many, and also in the presence of the fishermen who were first called by him. Their life-focused search for prosperity would in their time with Jesus's shift to a new search, one for the ultimate victory of "determinative will over formidable opposition," even though they might not have recognized that arc in quite that way in their earliest days with Jesus. Peter's dramatic and profound recognition of Jesus's divinity continued, but did not complete, his understanding, Jesus seeking, often with frustration, to expand it. In the end, Jesus addressing gathered assemblies, performing miracles, explaining, clarifying in quieter moments, all with personal courage repeatedly demonstrated, grew understandings. His resurrection should have grown it exponentially—so why, then, did these fishermen return to fishing in Galilee, where Jesus found them having returned to what they knew before they were called and had had their three-year experience in his presence?

Had the question of what to do next returned them to the lives they knew, and at a distance from the just-experienced dangers in Jerusalem? A comfort in the certainties of their yesteryears in contrast to the uncertainties of their tomorrows? Maybe both of those reasons in the shortness of days? But they were awaiting Jesus rejoining them, his guidance to them in the words of the Great Commission not forgotten but without the particulars, the details, of how to go about that task?

Following the near-total destruction of Jerusalem in 70 AD and the dispersal of most Jews, some managed to remain, though they were scattered over Galilee and Judea. Though they took a modicum of comfort in the fact that they had survived successive invaders and occupiers for centuries, their inescapable reality was they were suppressed and oppressed again, and at risk when gathering generally and greater risk if suspected of worship. The slow recovery of Judaism filled part of the void left by the demise of the Sadducees and the dispersal of the Pharisees. Early Christians witnessed the rise of their faith in Galilee and Judea, but what became Christianity did not flourish in either for several centuries.

Lest we believe wrongly that Galilee and Judea were insignificant subjugated lands compared to others within the empire, they were given significant attention in Rome. Vespasian became emperor of Rome while on military campaign in Judea and Roman Egypt, and his son and imperial successor Titus besieged and captured Jerusalem, destroying its Second Temple and, in larger measure, that metropolis. If you are touring Rome's Colosseum, read this inscription: "The Emperor Caesar Vespasian Augustus had this new amphitheater erected with the spoils of war," which include especially the sack of Jerusalem and its temple. It is but one example in Rome's environs. Nearly 2,000 years precludes us from attending a triumphant parade of booty and Jewish prisoners destined for ritual slaughter in the Colosseum, but a carved stonework depicting the Second Temple's huge menorah adorns the nearby Arch of Titus in celebration of that victory. Pompey the Great had earlier founded the ten cities known as the Decapolis to the east of the Sea of Galilee. What evidence these realities are that Galilee was not a provincial backwater! It was important in the corridors of Rome.

CHAPTER 4

Jesus, His Fishermen, and Their Fish

What thoughts and words conveying them can be added to scripture written by those who were contemporaries of Jesus and his fishermen and wrote authoritatively about him and them? The answer is: much. Christians too often believe that "If it's not in the Bible, it isn't true," when much truthful historical record does exist, ranging across contemporary Hebrew, Roman, Egyptian, and other written records, but we need to continue here from the scriptural passages which are tied most directly to this account of Jesus and his fishermen.

From Mark 1:

> As Jesus walked beside the Sea of Galilee, he saw Simon and his brother Andrew casting a net into the lake, for they were fishermen. "Come, follow me," Jesus said, "and I will send you out to fish for people." At once they left their nets and followed him. When he had gone a little farther, he saw James son

> of Zebedee and his brother John in a boat, preparing their nets. Without delay he called them, and they left their father Zebedee in the boat with the hired men and followed him.

From Matthew 16:

> When Jesus came to the region of Caesarea Philippi, he asked his disciples, "Who do people say the Son of Man is?" They replied, "Some say John the Baptist, others say Eliah, and still others, Jeremiah or one of the prophets." "But what about you?" he asked. "Who do you say I am? Simon Peter answered, "You are the Messiah, the Son of the living God." Jesus replied, "Blessed are you, Simon son of Jonah, for this was not revealed to you by flesh and blood, but by my Father in heaven. And I tell you, That you are Peter, and on this rock I will build my church, and the gates of Hades will not overcome it. I will give you the keys of the kingdom of heaven; whatsoever you bind on earth will be bound in heaven, and whatever you loose on earth will be loosed in heaven."

From Luke 5:

> One day as Jesus was standing by the Lake of Gennesaret [the Sea of Galilee], the people were crowding around him and listening to the word of God, He saw at the water's edge two boats, left there by the fishermen, who were washing their nets. He got into one of the boats, the one belonging to Simon,

and asked him to put out a little from the shore. Then he sat down and taught from the boat.

When he had finished speaking, he said to Simon, "Put out into deep water, and let down the nets for a catch."

Simon answered, "Master, we've worked hard all night and haven't caught anything. But because you say so, I will let down the nets."

When they had done so, they caught such a large number of fish that their nets began to break. So they signaled their partners in the other boat to come and help them, and they came and filled both boats so full they began to sink.

When Simon Peter saw this, he fell at Jesus' knees, and said, "Go away from me, Lord; I am a sinful man!" For he and all his companions were astonished at the catch of fish they had taken, and so were James and John, the sons of Zebedee, Simon's partners. Then Jesus said to Simon, "Don't be afraid; from now on you will fish for people. So they had pulled their boats up on shore, and followed him.

From John 6:

Some time after this, Jesus crossed to the far shore of the Sea of Galilee (that is, the Sea of Tiberias) [the Sea of Galilee], and a great crowd of people followed him because they saw the signs he had performed by healing the sick. Then Jesus went up on a mountainside and sat down with his disciples. The Jewish Passover Festival was near.

When Jesus looked up and saw a great crowd coming toward him, he said to Philip, "Where shall we buy bread for these people to eat?" He asked this only to test him, for he already had in mind what he was going to do.

Philip answered him, "It would take more than half a year's wages to buy enough bread for each one to have a bite!"

Another of his disciples, Andrew, Simon Peter's brother, spoke up: "Here is a boy with five small barley loaves and two small fish, but how far will they go among so many?"

Jesus said, "Have the people sit down." There was plenty of grass in that place, and they sat down (about five thousand men were there). Jesus then took the loaves, gave thanks, and distributed to those who were seated as much as they wanted. He did the same with the fish.

When they had all had enough to eat, he said to his disciples "Gather the pieces that are left over. Let nothing be wasted." So they gathered them and filled twelve baskets with the pieces of the five barley loaves left over by those who had eaten.

After the people saw the sign Jesus performed, they began to say "Surely this is the Prophet who is to come into the world." Jesus, knowing that they intended to make him king by force, withdrew again to the mountain by himself.

This was not an isolated event for, while Jesus miraculously fed 5000 in Tabgha, and he fed another 4000 several months later in Kursi.

From John 21:

> Afterward Jesus appeared again to his disciples, by the Sea of Galilee. It happened this way: Simon Peter, Thomas (also known as Didymus) Nathanael from Cana in Galilee, the sons of Zebedee, and two other disciples were together. "I'm going out to fish" Simon Peter told them, and they said, "We'll go with you." So they went out and got into the boat, but that night they caught nothing.
>
> Early in the morning, Jesus stood on the shore, but the disciples did not realize that it was Jesus.
>
> He called out to them, "Friends, haven't you any fish?"
>
> "No," they answered.
>
> He said, "Throw your net on the other right side of the boat and you will find some." When they did, they were unable to haul the net in because of the large number of fish.
>
> Then the disciple whom Jesus loved said to Peter, "It is the Lord!" As soon as Simon Peter heard him say, "It is the Lord," he wrapped his outer garment around him (for he had taken it off) and jumped into the water. The other disciples followed in the boat, towing the net full of fish, for they were not far from the shore, about a hundred yards. When they landed, they saw a fire of burning coals there with fish on it, and some bread.
>
> Jesus said to them, "Bring some of the fish you have just caught." So Simon Peter climbed back into the boat and dragged the net ashore. It was full of

> large fish, but even with so many the net was not torn. Jesus said to them, "Come and have breakfast." None of the disciples dared ask him, "Who are you?" They knew it was the Lord. Jesus came, took the bread and gave it to them, and did the same with the fish. This was now the third time Jesus appeared to his disciples after he was raised from the dead.

Together, these passages set out what we might not have recalled or at least promptly of Jesus's knowledge of fishermen, fishing and fish.

He gave now globally recognized presences in history to fishermen Peter, Andrew, James, and John. They became his innermost circle among twelve disciples, meaning learned followers, later in the Bible's narratives referred to as apostles, meaning advocates with authority from whomever sent them on their mission; in their instances, Jesus. Each was a fisher of fish who became a fisher of persons' souls. They became sometimes knowing and sometimes unknowing instruments through whose roles Jesus's powers were demonstrated to multitudes. The feeding of a multitude assembled to hear him demonstrates how he worked in ways to demonstrate his powers to his disciples, and it began with a boy's foresight to take lunch with him to a predictably large and long outdoor event.

This youngster brought his lunch to an assembly of thousands of men, whose number scripture informs us without counting the accompanying women and children gathered to hear Jesus. As Jesus and his perplexed disciples discussed how they could feed a crowd of so many, one had noted that the boy's lunch was the only food within sight. He gave his lunch over to Jesus's use and was probably as amazed as all others at what followed, but then was proud of his role. Little did he know his act would enter history, and we know he and his lunch meal were spotted by fishermen, Jesus's discussions about the situation were with those fishermen, and the miraculous multiplication was also of fish, not only of bread. Further, we know that Jesus knew the importance of fish to the daily sustenance of those who gathered to hear him. Because it is possible, perhaps probable, that others had also brought something for themselves to eat, why is the choice of the boy's so significant? Several commentators have responded that it was because he was, as a young boy, innocent of the presumed sins of the elders, that innocence a tie to what Jesus's ministry was seeking as the new way, his way.

At other times Jesus prepared and cooked fish in the presence of disciples he called from their boats. Beyond that ordinariness, he did what every fisher of fish has wished at some time, if not frequently, he could do: he commanded fish to gather into a school tight enough to be netted and taken into a boat, and the fish did. Furthermore, he directed the catching by Peter standing at the Sea of Galilee's water edge of a fish with a tribute coin for the temple in its mouth, an act so astonishing in its complexity, it is included in listings of Jesus's miracles and further demonstrated to his disciples his God-like power.

There can be little wonder why a symbol of the Christian faith in its earliest centuries was a simple diagram of a fish:

In addition to its identification with Jesus and his fishermen, it was so simple it could be drawn with only two movements of the toe end of a sandal in street or marketplace dust as a concealed and easily erased communication by one person to another.

Furthermore, the Greek word for fish, ΙΧΘΥΣ, spelled *ichthys* in the Latin alphabet, is the Greek acronym for "Jesus Christ, God's Son, Savior." We know this root word for it appears in ichthyology, the scientific study of fish. What some know less is that this fish symbol was not alone among the faith's early symbols.

They included another Greek alphabet–based description of Christ derived from that word's first two letters in Greek—an X and a P overlaid as a single image, pronounced chi-rho and appearing as:

☧

Chi-rho is the overlay of the first two capital letters of the Greek word ΧΡΙΣΤΟΣ, that being Christos. Additional symbols included a dove with an olive branch, a dove without a branch, a shepherd with a lamb across his shoulders, an anchor, a lyre, a praying person with outstretched arms, a ship, and a peacock, the latter a symbol of long or perpetual life. These images were worked into early church mosaics, many of which have survived. The fish and most others symbols were succeeded in houses of religious worship by the cross, for Jesus nailed to his is the most expressive of Jesus's death by agonizing crucifixion, it the worst possible form of execution. Excruciating pain from body weight pulling against large nails driven into wrists and feet or ankles, labored breathing, carnivorous birds claws and beaks pecking at eyes, flies everywhere there was blood on brow, face, and feet, altogether protracted agony, a profoundly graphic reminder of his sacrifice of self to atone for the sins of all persons. We will return to this.

In our secular era, the Jesus whom the voices from many pulpits wish the congregation to hear is that of an exceptionally ethical and talented equivalent of a social worker, but that facet, albeit significant in Jesus's own teachings as to a person's duties in day-to-day life, is subordinate to Jesus as the forgiver of sins and offeror of ever-lasting salvation. Both can be understood and appreciated, but Jesus the redeemer and savior is paramount.

The congregant or anyone else ought not to have an issue with that, for they are Jesus's admonitions to do what he has prioritized for lives lived then and those lived now. Unfortunately, sometimes this social service focus seems to be the most those pulpits wish us to know about Jesus and his relationship with each of us. That wish obscures a far greater takeaway from his life, and it is his sacrifice of himself by death as an actual, not figurative, atonement for the sins of each of the living, and the agony of his crucifixion.

Those who have heard or read scripture know the events described here, though they may not have given attention to the similarities in fishing for fish and fishing for converts to the emerging faith. They are worth noting:

- Fish do not come knowingly to fishers for the purpose of being captured.
- Fish cannot be compelled by anglers to come to a hand, a hook, or a net.
- Fish may be attracted to whatever bait is proffered, but they usually observe quite cautiously before deciding to take it.

These points are similar to persons, too, thus the second perspective:

> Humans cannot be compelled to truly believe inwardly, no matter what adherence they may be compelled to show outwardly for advancement or self-preservation.

There is much frustration in fishing for fish and fishing for religious converts, both engendering appreciation for the exercise of patience.

As a fisher has efforts which result in few or no fish, a fisher of persons has similar experiences, in both instances disappointing and frustrating, leaving both to think through and engage new strategies to increase prospects of future successes.

In the modern era, fishers abide by catch-and-release practices by which caught fish are returned to their waters with an exponential hope. Since time immemorial, religious teachers have asked believers to return to their families and neighbors to spread the word, an action embodying a hope for growth in the number of believers.

The importance of fishermen in the life of Jesus does not end here. It is magnified in an event which occurred only six days after Jesus's designation at Caesarea Philippi of Simon, by then renamed Simon Peter, following his "You are the Messiah" declaration made in Caesarea Philippi, an area known widely for its worship of false gods, as the leader of those who would carry forth Jesus's mission after an ascension about which these fishermen at that time knew nothing. This is a moment of unparalleled importance. Before those to whom he was entrusting the carrying on of his teachings, Jesus accepted the mantle of messiah, as foretold and in him embodied. He did so with the intent to move Judaism from centuries of continued anticipation of a messiah defined in King David's attributes to the prominence of the traditional Judaic features of the love of God, one's neighbors, strangers and enemies, that unifying theme expressed as long ago as Moses and Isaiah. Prophecy was fulfilled in a manner unforeseen in centuries of Jews looking backward to David to define the present instead of looking from the present forward in which these virtues were to be renewed in Judaism and brought new to the Gentiles. He had set into motion a revolution, but a spiritual one strengthened by words, not by the return of King David's swords of sharpened and hardened metal.

According to Matthew 17:

> After six days Jesus took with him Peter, James and John the brother of James, and led them up a high mountain by themselves. There he was transfigured before them. His face shone like the sun, and his clothes became as white as the light. Just then there appeared before them Moses and Elijah, talking with Jesus.
>
> Peter said to Jesus, "Lord, it is good for us to be here. If you wish, I will put up three shelters—one for you, one for Moses and one for Elijah."
>
> While he was still speaking, a bright cloud covered them, and a voice from the cloud said, "This is my Son, whom I love; with him I am well pleased. Listen to him!"

We know the importance of Jesus's transfiguration in the Christian faith for it is among the milestones in his life on Earth: miraculous conception, baptism, transfiguration, crucifixion, resurrection, ascension, and the leaving of the Holy Spirit with us. Christians regard these pillars as confirmations of his divinity. The transfiguration is one of only two miracle-like acts in Jesus's life that transformed him instead of transforming other persons, the second act being his resurrection. The transfiguration is a dividing line between his first two and a half years of preaching and performing of God-like miracles and what lay ahead in the handful of months left to him in his physical presence on Earth.

The work of Jesus and his fishermen continued, bringing his message to those who shared their Jewish faith, Jesus having first declared that he was sent only to the lost sheep of Israel. Yet, in his witnessing over time the presence of those who were not Jews among the assembled to see and hear him, and in his rewarding the depths of faith of the centurion from Capernaum and the hemorrhaging woman from Caesarea Philippi, neither of whom were Jewish, Jesus expanded his ministry to the Gentiles. Unlike the Jews who already had their covenant with God, Gentiles had none, but some among them sought such a covenant. In John 10:16, Jesus made his disciples aware of changes in his thinking:" I have other sheep that are not of this sheep pen. I must bring them also. They too will listen to my voice, and there shall be one flock and one shepherd." This was Jesus describing himself as the one shepherd not only of Jews but also of other flocks, a foretelling of the faith's vastly expanded future. He tested this widening by traveling to Sidon and Tyre in Phoenicia, only a long day's walk to the north from Galilee, and to the Decapolis communities east of the Sea of Galilee. These actions fulfilled the "sign of Jonah," noting Jonah's hometown of Gath Hepher having been only a short distance from where Nazareth was settled. What was this sign and its meaning? That, while the kingdom of heaven would first be offered to the Jews, those other than Jews would accept it and that acceptance would be a confirming sign that the prophesied messianic kingdom had begun. Demonstrations of that consequence are found in scripture and later early Christian history.

Following Jesus's resurrection and ascension, James the Just in Jerusalem became the head of a profession of Jewish faithful accepting of Jesus's proposed reforms within Judaism, while Peter became head of the church of the Gentiles built out in its earliest days by him, Paul, and others into a different, though not wholly apart, religious faith. That Christian faith became the world's largest by number of adherents, and the Jewish faith that was dispersed in large measure from Galilee and Judea as Roman rule intensified after its destruction of the Second Temple endured other Sho'ah (destruction), grew and prospered in exile, and returned in enlarging numbers as a consequence of diplomatic and other initiatives in the wake of the 1933–1945 European Sho'ah, which Christians know as the holocaust.

We can see by these descriptions, and in Matthew 17, Mark 9, and Luke 9, why Jesus's transfiguration was and is a particular source of pride to fishermen. Peter, James the son of Zebedee, and John his brother, and no other disciples, were chosen by Jesus to accompany him to this metamorphosizing event connecting this world and another, the temporal and eternal.

CHAPTER 5

The River Jordan and Its Sea of Galilee

Knowing this river and this inland sea is central to understanding the ministry of Jesus. Each is far more than a geographical reference.

Even though ancient Israel was in westernmost Asia, also known as Asia Minor, even with that clarifier it was only marginally in Asia. By contrast, in the eyes of today's world community, modern Israel is unquestionably in the Middle East.

By whatever name or reference, most observers do not think of its array of ancient and modern cities surrounded by wildernesses and water in respect to fish or fishing. They should, for there are old and new accounts on fishing in the Mediterranean, the Sea of Galilee, the River Jordan and elsewhere in the region. Maps in our childhood school rooms showed abundant fresh water in that Sea of Galilee and elsewhere and salt water at Israel's west coast and southern-most tip at a finger of the Red Sea. There are no fish, at least not yet, in the heavily salted Dead Sea, the River Jordan's southern terminus. We were enthralled as youngsters by imagining what it would be like to float on the latter's surface. Those classes' maps and books informed us of Israel's rivers, other lakes, and tunnels even in ancient times connecting water from underground pools to communities. There were ports bustling with commercial trade, including the export of processed fish, at ancient Israel's docks on the Mediterranean, nautical gateways to Greece, Rome and elsewhere.

Freshwater fish are caught mostly at the Sea of Galilee, it being the up-to-eight-mile-wide midsection of the River Jordan, and at other sites in Israel's 8,000 square miles. That total square mileage is about 1,300 less than New Hampshire's. The southernmost tip of Israel reaches the Gulf of Aqaba, a narrow finger of the Red Sea, which stretches southward to the Gulf of Aden, and it in turn mixes with the Arabian Sea, and it with the Indian Ocean. Saltwater fish were then and are now caught in such open waters. The freshwater and saltwater fish species in and near Israel are believed to vary only slightly from those of the time of Jesus.

The Jordan and its tributaries, as well as its mid-course Sea of Galilee and the Dead Sea where it ends as a contained basin, add immeasurably to the distinctive character of Galilee. The river rises from three sites, they being the sources of the Dan, Hazbani, and Banias tributaries toward Mount Hermon and Transjordan in Israel's northernmost stretches. What implies by its name a single mount at Hermon is actually a forty-three-mile mountainous cluster straddling Israel's borders with Syria and Lebanon, a cluster described by scholar Ernest Masterman as "a confused mass of tumbled mountains" of which Mount Hermon is a pinnacle among them. The Hebrew word *hermon* can be defined as the "mountain set apart" as it is in Matthew 17. Its meaning is drawn from the Semitic root *hrm*, which means consecrated, and the Arabic *al-haram*, meaning sacred enclosure. Eusebius Caesarea, fourth-century bishop of Caesarea Maritima during which Caesarea and Jerusalem had respectable libraries and he was himself a learned Christian, wrote in his *Onomasticon*, a directory of faith-tied place names, that Mount Hermon was respected by nations of peoples as a sacred place. We gather by his and other accounts why the Jordan, too, was an important site in biblical descriptions of places, events, and persons. This is the bishop who read the once-local-to-only-the-Caesarea creed of belief to those participating in the 325 AD Council of Nicaea, which text became, after considered deliberation, the Nicene Creed that defined Christianity for believers to believe and others to know.

Renowned for its pure water from winter snows and pristine cloud formations, Mount Hermon has been known colloquially as the mountain of snow, the snowy mountain, and the gray-haired mountain. It is the source of essential dew clouds which in late summer descend southward onto Israel's fields of grain, grapes, figs, and olives and, in doing that, contribute to better harvests. In modern Israel, this range is known as "the eyes of the nation" for the more than 9,000-foot elevation makes it Israel's primary early warning sector of any military action in or coming from Lebanon or Syria. Mount Hermon's southern slopes extend into the Golan Heights, reacquired by Israeli military action in the Six-Day War of 1967 and expanded by it in the Yom Kippur War of 1973. I have walked along part of the Golan Heights border fence between Israel and Syria, astonished by the panoramic look down from that elevation over nearly all of Israel with Syria and Jordan to the left, and the Mediterranean to the right.

North of the Sea of Galilee is what remains of Lake Hula (also called Huleh), lying between the Golan Heights to its east and the Upper Galilee mountains to its west. It may have been here that, citing Isaiah 52 and 53 and Psalm 22, that Jesus told his disciples that he was going to be killed but in three days would arise from his death. It became evident to him, when they had reached Peter's mother-in-law's house in Capernaum, that the disciples still did not, or seemed not, to comprehend what he was setting out and its enormous importance to him, them, and the history of humankind.

Among Hebrews the Jordan is known as Ha-Yarden and its history long tied to their presence. For Christians, a particular site has exceptional importance. It is near the southern end of its stretch between the Sea of Galilee and the Dead Sea and is at Yardenit, known also as Qasr el Yahud. It is widely regarded as the site of John the Baptist's baptism of Jesus. Scripture informs us this is the site of the descending of the Spirit upon Jesus, attesting to his divine nature, and initiating his teaching through preaching and healing. His baptism was in and by water, a fluid available to even the poorest of the poor in contrast with the frankincense- and myrrh-scented oils that anointed Jesus's ancestor David and others of wealth and power and were brought to the infant Jesus in Bethlehem. In an arid land, it may be a stretch to refer to water as ubiquitous, but it is when contrasted with precious oils.

Except for its Sea of Galilee wide midsection, the Jordan is narrow during three of each year's four seasons. It begins down steep descents in the north, then widens as it moves toward the Sea of Galilee and becomes for thirteen miles of length that inland sea, described by some as the world's holiest lake. Gustaf Dalman, the German orientalist and Lutheran theologian, captured that conclusion in his *Sacred Sites and Ways* with these words: "If anywhere, here by the lake we were in the very home of Christianity." It is the largest naturally occurring freshwater lake in the Middle East south of modern Turkey's borders. Farther south, near the site of Jesus's baptism, a stone can be thrown across the river except during spring runoff's wider flow.

While the Jordan is 223—sometimes-meandering—miles long, a straight line from its farthest source to where it enters the Dead Sea is less than 125 miles. While the sea's maximum depth fluctuates between periods of heavy rainfall and its runoffs on one hand and droughts on the other, it is roughly 130 feet, which is fairly shallow and about the length of a typical modern office building's single hallway. It is the lowest freshwater lake and the second-lowest of all lakes in the world, the Dead Sea to its immediate south and to which its waters flow being the lowest.

Understanding the Jordan requires knowing its course from the mountains to the Dead Sea. As it flows from those mountain's foothills, it has an irregular flow of twists and turns through ravines which constitute many miles of its length. Then, its descent is more gradual, even sluggish, as it winds through meadow like terrain until it reaches the fords of King David's and World War I British General Edmund Allenby's times. Its course here has little visibility from a distance, but up close, you know it is there because its seeped water sustain poplars and willows in spring with summer greens and autumn's yellows and browns. Thick shrubbery under them adds to its visibility.

Where the river course meets the Sea of Galilee, there are large patches of sturdy brown reeds growing to nearly fifteen feet and once highly valued to be woven between the beams and crossbeams of house ceilings of Jesus's time to reinforce the weight of compacted mud dried and fired as roofing. Huts to protect persons from the elements and fences to contain fowl, goats, and other farmyard animals were built using them as reinforcement rods. If "a hut is not a house" were said by its owner in those times, it may have been to a priest or a tax collector, for a hut was not subjected to either the temple tithe or the government tax at the higher rate of a house. These reeds were marketed as far south as Jerusalem, and some scholars speculate that the reed put into Jesus's hand as a scepter at his crucifixion to mock his kingship of the Jews may have been one of these reeds.

Winter rains raise the water level of the Sea of Galilee, expanding its surface area, appreciably when there has been much rainfall. The difference between winter's lowest temperature and summer's highest is dramatic, felt in the air and in the water. For a mostly arid region, winter rains were and remain important to fisheries, agriculture, and husbandry. Before the modern age's linguistic differentiations, the Arabic word for rain was used synonymously with the word winter, for they were conjoined in the mind's reflections on that season's weather.

Like most rivers, the Jordan has narrow and broad stretches, typically narrowest at their origins and broadest at their mouths. The Jordan is different. It is narrow, then wide, then much wider as the Sea of Galilee, then returns to narrow for its final stretch to the larger Dead Sea basin at which it ends. Nature and man have reconfigured its pattern over the past century. To try in springtime to swim across its strong currents is dangerous and to wade across impossible. In autumn it is possible to swim across all but its Sea of Galilee stretch and in numerous locations both low and slow enough to be forded.

The Jordan becomes the Sea of Galilee and the widest eight miles south of the confluence at which it meets the lake, returning at its lower course to only a river's width in the stretch now dividing Israel and the Palestinian territories. From there it flows toward the Dead Sea at 1,412 feet below sea level, "making its shores the lowest land-based elevation on Earth" and its 997-foot water depth, owing to its tectonic origins, "the deepest hypersaline lake in the world" among a handful from the Caspian Sea to Djibouti and to Antarctica.

Known in Hebrew as *Yam ha-Melah,* that is "Sea of Salt," the name Dead Sea not appearing in the Bible, it does appear in Genesis 14:3 by reference to the valley of Siddim. What was once Sodom is on its southwestern shore. Mention of the Dead Sea recalls the site of caves at nearby Qumran in which scrolls of religious texts, including a nearly complete body of Hebrew Scripture, were secreted for their protection from adversarial authorities, most probably the Romans of 70AD and the years immediately following, the scrolls known today as the Dead Sea Scrolls. The hiding of scrolls in caves in the face of impending war and other turmoil was a well-established tactic for avoiding their destruction. It is not unthinkable that those fleeing to Masada hid them here for it is in that direction. In the vast research which followed their discovery, scholars noted that the texts included every book in today's Hebrew Bible except one, the Esther. The most frequently found of the restored scrolls is that of Psalms (*Tehillim*, meaning praises in Hebrew), presumably because of its theme on the power of God as an interventionist savior. This sea was well known from history and personal experiences in Jesus's time, and Herod the Great even had his own resort there.

The starkness of the Dead Sea's adjective reflects a saline content so high that habituated life beyond microbial does not survive in its water. Its surface is 3.6 times larger than the Sea of Galilee's owing to their distinct geological basins and the Israeli government's dam-regulated outflow of rising waters in the Sea of Galilee to avoid commercial and residential damage from too high seasonal levels. From where did its salt come? It's worth the knowing.

What is now the basin holding the Jordan's Sea of Galilee and its downstream Dead Sea was most probably an estuary of the Mediterranean Sea at its west, a basin flooded by the Mediterranean's salty waters over geological time. As the tectonic rift running up from East Africa pushed in that time this 230-mile Jordan Rift Valley upward, or compressing tectonic plates created a step-over, or both occurred, its waterway to the Mediterranean was closed off, leaving most of its water to evaporate. There is another reason too: as the lowest level on Earth, there was no lower level into which its water could flow. The average salinity of oceans and saline seas is 3 percent to 4 percent, that salt being 85 percent sodium chloride, which approximates the chemical composition we recognize and use as table salt. Dead Sea salt is only 30 percent sodium, but it is prized for its uses, among others in healthcare and beauty formulations. It is a significant product with commercial interests tied to those and recreational uses. That observation moves this focus from the time of Jesus and his fishermen to our time.

Concerns over the continuing concentration of Dead Sea salt caused a recent Jordanian–Israeli–Palestinian study to be undertaken to determine the feasibility of building a tunnel-and-pipe system to bring less saline water from the Mediterranean, the rising level of which is threatening its own shorelines, to the Dead Sea. The proposed project would have generated both hydroelectric power and income to cover costs of construction, operation, and maintenance, but the report determined the proposal not to be feasible. Opposition to the proposal came from at least four directions: sensitivities over the intended multinational partnership; current recreational and other commercial operations tied to harvesting its salt; environmentalists seeking to protect the sea's natural state and appearance; and those wary of its possible fulfillment of an ancient end-of-days prophecy.

The latter opposition may have been derived from a sixth-century BC one found in Ezekiel 47:10: "Fishermen will stand along the shore; from En Gedi to En Eglaim, there will be places for spreading nets. The fish will be of many kinds—like the fish of the Mediterranean Sea." This is the Ezekiel whose words are inscribed on the Monument to Holocaust survivors at Jerusalem's Yad Vashem Shoah memorial to the twentieth-century holocaust. It is the Ezekiel of the chariots of fire, his "wheels within wheels" vision recorded as

> I looked and saw a whirlwind coming from the north, a great cloud with fire flashing back and forth and brilliant light all around it. In the center of the fire was a glow like amber, and within it was the form of four living creatures. And this was their appearance. They had a human form,

which description readers regard with respect even if not wholly understanding it. When the reasons for not proceeding further with the project were reported publicly, it is possible that hopes of prolonging the number of years before the Dead Sea had been restored gave additional weight to the decision. For some of that time, Michelangelo's painting of Ezekiel in the Vatican's Sistine Chapel will continue to stare toward God's finger touching Adam's. Perhaps in time this tunnel-and-pipe project or a similar one will be undertaken.

The Jordan's upstream Sea of Galilee is on the other hand a freshwater lake. Tributaries and fresh water and saline-tainted springs have fed it for thousands of years. Its water level varies as steadier rainfall and winter runoff raise it, while summer heat's evaporation, prolonged droughts, and water drawn for agricultural irrigation reduce it. A huge pumping station to the west of Tabgha and sitting atop Tel Kinnerot, which was once the principal town of the tribe of Naphtali, draws water from the lake for its distribution throughout much of Israel.

For nearly a century, its level has been regulated also by the floodgates of the Degania Dam where its water begins the Jordan's concluding stretch to the Dead Sea. This dam was completed in the early 1930s as part of a hydroelectric power plant project, but it is not without continued controversy. In fact, the question, "What to do this time?" nearly every annual cycle requires an answer combining hydrological and politics. While a higher water level supports agricultural and other uses by assuring water's continued availability for drawdowns, it threatens shoreline properties and their commercial interests. On the other hand, the higher level's greater weight suppresses the infusion of saline water from some of its underwater springs, a suppression which helps to maintain fresh water purity. Dilemma upon dilemma, but this is not the only unusual aspect of the lake.

Rather startlingly, a 2013 archaeological report disclosed an elongated cone-shaped cairn, a traditional construction of heavy stones over a burial site, one hidden in this instance well below the lake's surface. It is a massive formation of a thirty-two-foot height, 230-foot diameter, and calculated 60,000-ton weight. It is on its western lake bed about a mile south of Tiberias's shoreline. That tonnage is heavier than many modern warships, and that diameter is twice that of England's Stonehenge. It consists of unhewn, naturally faced, basalt boulders and cobbles with no sign of cutting or chiseling. Believed to be more than 4,000 years old, neither its origin is known nor its conjectured purpose publicly disclosed by the government of Israel. It is a matter of public wonderment as to what the cairn covers in that its location presumes it was constructed on the lakebed when it was dry land. Collapsed basalt formations can occur naturally from the rapid cooling of low-viscosity lava.

When I drive eastward from Bethlehem or Jerusalem to Jericho, I pass a roadside marker indicating that I am going lower than the Mediterranean Sea level nearly fifty miles (eighty kilometers) to my back. This marker is not far from the site identified in the parable of the Good Samaritan. Jericho is one of the oldest continuously inhabited cities, extending back at least 9,000 years, with the oldest surviving protective wall in the world. The old and the recent walls are more than 800 feet (240 meters) below sea level and look westward to the Mount of Temptation from the scriptural account of Jesus in the wilderness, which barren land extends along the descent from the high plateau of Judea into the Jordan valley of which Jericho is one of many ancient sites. That wilderness is where Jesus resisted and rebuked temptations for forty days. Why was he subjecting himself to this intense period of deprivation and temptation? Because he was on Earth as a person filled with the range of free will encountering human experience to yield or reject its many manifestations. Jesus prevailed and returned from the Jordan and the wilderness to Galilee to preach adherence to the Law of Moses and demonstrate resistance to temptation, repentance for that not resisted, reconciliation, and the religion-based faith overarching all in marked contrast to violations of that law by yielding to temptation and ignoring its consequences.

The Sea of Galilee was known in Jesus's time and is even now by different names, they reflecting a once dominant settlement on its shores and the language of each people but each referring to the same body of water. Hebrew-Aramaic and other references over millennia are to the lake of Kinneret and Kinnereth, from *kinnor,* meaning harp, that being its shoreline appearance when seen from above. An indigenous Hebrew designation for it in Jesus's time was Yam Ginnesar and Yamma de-Ginnesar. Driving past or walking its shoreline, I bear in mind that in Hebrew and in Aramaic, *yam* can mean either sea or lake, translations from Matthew, Mark, and John referencing it as a sea and from Luke as a lake. The names Gennesaret and Ginosar may have derived from the valley in which to "guard" or "watch against" an invasion of Judea from the north. Reference to it as a sea is the more common choice among English-speaking Christian writers, perhaps because a sea seems bigger than a lake and, additionally, there is the safeguard of other inland lakes also known as seas. The Caspian Sea, south of the Russian steppes in easternmost Europe and north of the Iranian plateau of western Asia, and the Aral Sea, surrounded by Kazakhstan and Uzbekistan, are also referred to as seas. Old Testament references to it begin in Deuteronomy's second millennium BC accounts and follow in Joshua.

Explorations of its biblical-era fishing ports during the severe 1980s drought's reduction of its water level confirmed how well the evangelists knew its villages, harbors, and put-in sites. The Roman name for it was the Sea of Tiberias in recognition of the emperor, and had come later in time to be used alongside the earlier Greek name Auton. Lake Tiberias adjoined the city of Tiberias named so by Herod Antipas, this naming a political gesture to the Roman emperor's ultimate authority over his and his brother Philip's lands. Herod Antipas made Tiberias his capital city, and its ruins lay today near the modern city of that name and its roughly 50,000 inhabitants.

When I cross the Allenby Bridge to travel from Jerusalem to Amman, Jordan, there are immigration and border security delays, as it is an exit point of Palestinians among others on the West Bank headed into Jordan, and an entry point into Israel when returning. A bridge at this location, which has steep banks, was built in 1918 at the direction of the British general who became a field marshal and later 1st Viscount Allenby. When Allenby became aware of its placement, the remains of a destroyed Ottoman bridge were here. Edmund Henry Hynman Allenby was more in early twentieth-century history of geographical Palestine than a conceptualizer of a sturdy bridge for vehicular traffic. In September 1918 and near the fortress of Megiddo in the Jezreel Valley, his cavalry units prevented the northward retreat of the Turkish 7th and 8th armies after his infantry had defeated them on the coastal plain. His overall operations led to the defeat of the Turks in the Middle East and contributed to the fall of the Ottoman Empire.

Allenby's place in military history as it related to the naming by others and the bridge's location could not stop this bridge from being destroyed by a 1927 earthquake. Rebuilt, it was destroyed again in 1946 during the Night of the Bridges paramilitary campaign of the Palmach, the elite arm of the Haganah, the underground armed force of the Jewish opposition to the British Mandate for Palestine, which authority lasted until 1948. Rebuilt again, it was destroyed in the 1967 Six-Day War. Rebuilt lastly in 1994 by the Japanese government as a commitment to the Norway-facilitated Oslo Accords' hopes of reducing Israeli–Palestinian disputes, it is now a modern bridge testifying to a failed hope of no further warfare in the area. That testimony did not deter a 2025 attack at it in which two Israeli soldiers were killed. It bears this Allenby Bridge name on the Israeli bank of the Jordan, but it is known at its eastern entrance into Israel as the King Hussein Bridge. By its very nature as a water course, there are fish along it, but perhaps because of maximum security barriers at and near the bridge and its border crossing station, I have never seen, whether looking north or south, anyone fishing the stream flowing under it.

There are many fish in the Sea of Galilee. When the water level is low from poor rainfall in its tributaries of which the Jordan is not the only water source, and with underwater springs adding to its volume, the sea's perimeter is thirty-two miles. A winter of significant rain fall will heighten its water level by two to three feet, causing the circumferential shoreline to be lengthened. It is said that its water was clearer in Jesus's time, but that cannot be assured given the number and nature of communities surrounding it and the presence of planted and grazed fields which drain toward it. Standing on the Golan Heights northeast of the lake and at Israel's Syrian border, one can see across the breadth and most of the length of modern Israel's footprint. It is one of the reasons why travel in Israel is easier than anticipated, for places known from history are closer to other places known, sometimes surprisingly closer.

Knowledge of the Jordan is more widely known in America than one might expect. Inspired by its themes of freedom from enslavement in scriptural passages from Genesis to Numbers, the lyrics of black spirituals, including "Deep River," "Wings Over Jordan," and "Roll, Jordan, Roll," give choral voice to that theme as does "On Jordan's Bank." In the 1870s Fisk University's Jubilee Singers, those students attending that historically black institution, toured the United States and Europe to raise funds to save the university from closing. They did so successfully. The lyrics of "Deep River" captured their hope for the long-sought peace of heaven reached by campgrounds along the way to freedom. The concept of crossing the Jordan to reach freedom was a thinly veiled reference to runaway slaves crossing the Ohio and other boundary rivers between slave states and free states, the song's imagery paralleling the textual imagery of Harriet Beecher Stowe's *Uncle Tom's Cabin*:

Oh, don't you want to go to that Gospel-feast,
That promis'd land where all is peace?
Lord, I want to cross over into campground.
I'll go into heaven, and take my seat,
Cast my crown at Jesus's feet.
Lord, I want to cross over into campground.
Oh, when I get to heav'n, I'll walk all about,
There's nobody there for to turn me out.
Lord, I want to cross over into campground.

This song sung by enslaved Africans in America echoed the cries for freedom of the Hebrews enslaved in pharaonic Egypt long before.

CHAPTER 6

Jesus in Nazareth and Galilee

Many of the highlights of Jesus's ministry occurred at and near the Sea of Galilee. They include his calling of others to join him in his mission, his teachings as to why they should, and the miracles which dramatically highlighted that mission. All followed a period as a newborn in Bethlehem to its south, an infancy of unknown length in farther south Egypt, and a youngster's maturity into adulthood. In contrast to this knowledge, we seldom reflect on the day-to-day nature of his life in Nazareth. According to Luke, Mary and Joseph lived there before his birth, but Matthew posits also that they came to Nazareth after their return from Egypt in order to fulfill the prophecy that the messiah would be a Nazarene. To harmonize those perspectives, it is possible that while Joseph and Mary had lived in Nazareth before Jesus's birth, they were uncertain about returning to it immediately given their concern over Herod the Great's homicidal animosity toward a foretold future king of the Jews, we recalling that was Herod's title given by the Roman Senate, not given by Jews. We also know both that

Herod's pompous and cruel son Herod Archelsus ruled Judea but not Galilee, which was ruled by his relatively more reasonable-appearing brother Antipas. We know also Joseph's occupation and that its uncertain income as an itinerant builder did not require him or his family to live in any particular place as long as he could undertake work where it was available.

It's worth noting that the Hebrew word for Christians, *Notzrim*, and the Arab word for them, *Nassara*, derive directly from Nazareth's associations with Jesus. The origin of the word Nazareth is tied to Jesus's Davidic clan's return from Babylon around 150 BC to 100 BC as most coming to Nazareth belonged to the Nazarene clan, known also as Natzoreans. These are important contexts for Jesus growing up among his own clan, but here is an even more important one as to where this occurred in the town of Nazara, *Nezer* in Hebrew, the both as Nazareth. This is tied to Old Testament prophecy and, when we hear it read in the Christian liturgical calendar, we misunderstand what it means in its tying to that prophecy. Matthew 2:23 informs us with: "So was fulfilled what was said through the prophets that he would be called a Nazarene." That which Matthew had in mind is found in Isaiah 11:1, in the prophetic announcement of the messiah: "A shoot will come up from the stump of Jesse, from his roots a Branch will bear fruit." Jesse was the father of King David, thus an offspring expressed as a "shoot" or "sprout," and would be from the house of David. What is the Hebrew word for such shoot or sprout? *Nezer*.

Nazareth was a small and relatively new village. Archaeologists generally agree that, in Jesus's lifetime, it was only about a hundred years to 150 years old with a population of fewer than 400 persons, perhaps even less, maybe half that. Its earliest written mention is in the Gospels, which is not surprising, for even the major urban hub of nearby Sepphoris is not mentioned in the Bible. The village was narrow at less than a half a mile in length and less than about a fifth of a mile in width, this exacting calculation based on the distances which an ancient Jewish village had to be from tombs—in Nazareth's instance from twenty-three of them. Important to the life of Jesus as well as to the village, it was at a welcomed distance from Roman and Jewish authorities in Jerusalem, enabling it to be regarded there of neither consequence nor threat to their interests. Those authorities' early awareness of Jesus of Nazareth, *Yeshua ha-Nozri*, which is how he would have been referred to in their discussions, as well as *Yeshua ben-Yosef* (Joshua son of Joseph), and his ministry were disregarded by them in part for these reasons of Nazareth's insignificant size and remoteness from Jerusalem. Yeshua is the shortened form of the Hebrew Yehōshu'a, meaning "Yahweh is salvation," that is, God is salvation. Thus, Jesus is the Greek translation of Yeshua.

Early written references to Nazareth not tied to Jesus and the advent of Christianity are rare. Even the nearly sole chronicler of that time, Flavius Josephus, gave it only a passing reference as a village where he had once stayed overnight to guard from it the roads from Galilee to the south. Epiphanius, the fourth-century scholar and Christian bishop of Salamis on Cyprus, reported tiny Nazareth as a purely Jewish locality. Jesus was educated in Hebrew scripture, and later rabbinical sources suggest that a synagogue school for young boys, a *Beth Midrash*, might have existed there. Further evidence indicates there was a synagogue constructed with its doors open to the direction of the Temple in Jerusalem in order that all Jews turned in prayer toward it. Muslims at prayer facing Mecca were not the first to have such a directional aspect in their worship.

Social customs arising from daily activities intersected at the village courtyard's shared clay oven for the baking of the culinary mainstay of bread. The Roman Catholic Basilica of the Annunciation, a modern construction built over the ruins of Byzantine and later Crusader churches, covers the site of a grotto- or cave-connected stone house in which Mary is said to have received the news from Gabriel that she would give birth to the divine Jesus. The Greek Orthodox Church of the Annunciation has been built at the site of Mary's Well, it already a modernized representation of the well visited by Mary and her kinswomen. It's important to note that differently named pilgrimage destinations, each with a supporting narrative, are found in many instances in the Holy Land. Here, a single or several wells were the only water sources for Galilean villages not located on or near flowing streams, and their springtime waters often ended by summer when other springs continued to flow abundantly.

In addition to its houses and wells, there was a Roman-era winepress, an olive press, and families' enclosures for domesticated animals. Jesus's Nazareth had three watchtowers, the dated remains of which confirm they existed in the late Hellenistic and early Roman years in order to assure that guards could look over vineyards subject to theft of grapes.

Most Nazareth homes were small and essentially cubic, constructed without any foundation other than hard-packed soil beneath it. They were built of more-or-less uniformly sized and stacked field stones joined by their weight and ample mortar mixed with lime extracted from the area's abundant limestone. Some were plastered with an external layer of mortar to resist destabilizing weakening over time from the effects of rain and wind. Most were four-walled, but some were three-walled if they adjoined a cave's or a grotto's open face. Some evidence and legend indicate that Mary and Joseph's habitation was one so built. Without stone floors and with few ornamentations, these houses were plain but functional.

Multigenerational families could add a room or two, usually moving outward, less seldom upward, but sometimes in an L- or squared U-shaped pattern to enable the laying of a patio whose floor could be soil or preferably stone, cobbles or molded bricks to eliminate or reduce rainy season mud. Houses' flat roofs, reached by outside ladders, could be terraced for the common practice of sleeping under the stars and were slightly slanted to collect valuable rainwater runoff. Two of the interior walls might have rectangular benches at their bases and shelving above them.

Accessory structures would have been daub-walled, a mud-and-straw mixture spread thickly across both sides of interwoven thin branches or Galilean reeds, or both, and then heat-hardened by torches held close to their surfaces. These out-buildings' walls required frequent repairs, as did houses, but they accomplished the purposes of sheltering equipment and supplies and confining small livestock. Night sounds in the neighborhood would have emanated from weather, neighboring houses and animals, including from the latter's necklaced bells. The elective physiological alarm for rising earlier or later the next morning would have been how much or how little water was drunk before sleep, a practice which remote populations in the world still follow. Compared to Galilean and Judean cities, Nazareth was a relatively quiet place, one in which personal privacy occurred only by awareness, request, absence, or distance.

A house's entrance had a jug whose water was reserved for ritual purification before entry. Inside, light would have been dim, during daytime entering primarily through an open doorway. Scant light at nighttime would have come from the wicks of seldom more than one or two small olive oil pottery lamps, light needed inside aided by summer's longer days and all seasons' moonlight. Natural surroundings provided some of the foodstuffs necessary for their lives, while gardens and fields added cultivated crops, but persistent poverty was ennobled and even oft-expressed as an act of faith.

Let us consider several observations concerning Jesus's family life not routinely considered. We know less about Jesus's father Joseph than we do about his mother, but we can build on what we do know to explore what may be discerned. Joseph was known in several contexts. Among his neighbors he was known as a *Tzaddik*, a righteous man who observed the law and applied it to day-to-day questions from the community in the absence of a rabbi's availability to do so. He is most often referred to as a carpenter, in Mark and Matthew as the carpenter, but that characterization is too narrow to capture fully what he did occupationally. It is relevant to this point that Greek and Latin were used frequently and had influences in Galilee.

The word used in respect to Joseph's occupation in Greek texts of Scripture, *tekton,* is closer in meaning to builder than to carpenter. We recognize it as the root word in English of architect, "a person who is qualified to design buildings and to plan and supervise their construction." Joseph and Jesus were carpenters who added other elements of building to their wood working, for they were considered in some rabbinic and early Christian writings to have been workers in related wood and stone. The Protoevangelium of James indicates this, even though this book is widely known to have accuracy issues. Beyond carpenters' work on buildings, including the preparation and installation of roof-beams to stabilize walls, crossbeams to support internal ceiling and external roofing, and doors for privacy and security, they would have made household furnishings—tables, benches, bedframes, trunks, boxes, and pails—and shaped and repaired hardwood plows and yokes. In each of these endeavors, to earn wages, they had to pay careful attention to details, a transferred attribute in Jesus's ministry.

In the strict social hierarchy of Joseph's and Jesus's time, those engaged in manual labor were regarded as having little more social status than peasants and slaves, because much of the work engaged in by free craftsmen was also done by slaves trained in their respective skills before or after their enslavement. True though that me be, neither Joseph nor Jesus fit solely into that building trades status, for father and son were qualified as well for answering villagers' questions about the application of Jewish law to everyday circumstances. That should have bolstered their credibility among their neighbors.

The Gospels relate Jesus's references to the laying the foundation of a house, the erection of a tower, and even the building of the Temple, but never to whether there was any of his or his father's handiwork in these endeavors. One scholar's explanation is that his life and spirit were simply never enclosed in the narrow confines of an artisan. Jesus knew the lives of the poor and how to speak with them of their needs and anxieties because he was from among them. He had common and profound human experiences in his earthly life, and as to them he stressed, distinguishing the spiritual from the material, that in God's kingdom life is earned by thought, word and deed, not by purchase.

One would think the need for the diversity of a carpenter's or a builder's finished products was enough to sustain a Nazareth-based livelihood, but it was not. This lack of a steady flow of work required Joseph to acquire additional skills and offer elsewhere what he knew how to do locally. He could have lived intermittently in Jerusalem where there was much ancillary work tied to the building of the Second Temple, but it was more distant than other opportunities. He may have worked in Sepphoris, only a handful of miles and an hour to an hour-and-a-half walk northwest of Nazareth. There was much work to be done there, for its rebuilding begun by Herod Antipas only a year after its 4 BC destruction, required a palace, courts, arsenals, market places, a theater, a prison, and many houses. Nazarenes went to it to buy and sell, borrow money and repay it, and pay taxes. It was a district religious center too, one with eighteen synagogues. Sepphoris is believed by some to have been the hometown of the mother of Jesus, thus Mary and Joseph could have either first met there, had several or joint first awareness of one another there, or been introduced there by a third party. If still alive and physically capable, Joseph may have worked in Tiberias to which Herod Antipas had moved his capital around 18 AD to 20 AD. Inasmuch as sons typically followed their father's occupation, a then time-honored but limiting rib of economic and social structures, Jesus could have accompanied his father to its work sites during the period of time about which the Bible is silent.

Sepphoris could be important for another reason. While Nazareth was a small village, albeit not shut off from the larger world close to it, its proximity to Sepphoris and the probability of visits to his mother's family and for work with his father would have overcome the risk of social isolation in Nazareth and any uneasiness with social goings on in larger spaces. It was a socialization step toward the enormity of Jerusalem.

While we have Gospel-based knowledge of the highlights of Jesus's ministry, we have less knowledge of his daily life, but we can reflect on what we do know. He traveled significant distances on foot, later accompanied by followers, only some of whose names Scripture informs us. They ate, slept, and undertook much else on daily, weekly, and annual cycles. They did that in communities where they knew persons in whose homes they shared meals and in whose homes or adjacent structures they slept. It was common to sleep on flat rooftops in both pleasant weather and when too hot to sleep inside.

Like others with him, Jesus would have been tired, his feet sore from walking on uneven terrain, sidestepping stones and dodging such shrubby growth as skin-irritating hawthorn and oleander, and seeking occasional shade at clumps of chaste trees. He would have been thirsty and hungry. He would have looked forward to resting at day's end and to discussions by dying embers with those accompanying him. Some of those discussions, but far from all, are set out in the New Testament, others appearing in apocryphal texts. In morning, their hair, clothes, and sacks would have smelled of the previous evening's campfire smoke, but they were accustomed to that sense from daily and nightly home hearths. In this terrain, he would have encountered the thorny *Ziziphus spina-christi*, that scientific name given centuries later in recognition of its use by Roman soldiers as his crown of thorns preceding and at his crucifixion. Not to be overlooked in considering that crowning is this species had long covered holy tombs.

What Jesus and those accompanying him carried by way of personal and shared items would almost certainly have been in woven woolen sacks slung over their shoulders. Where they traveled most was at least in part a Jewish land. In that, they had cultural comfort. Provisions for their time between settlements would have been gifts of bread, fruits, and raw vegetables, perhaps occasionally cured meats, dried fish, and even honey for which Galilee had a widespread reputation, but less frequently gifts of coin from poor or marginal middle-class families. These would have been sometimes suspenseful walks, for big cats and wild boars roamed these areas. They were areas which thirty years later Flavius Josephus as a commander of an infantry regiment would fortify against

Roman legions. Jesus would not have sought or expected much, for he was not accustomed to having much, and he followed the commandment's proscription against envy of material things. We know also that he had a range of human emotions, experiencing joy at the wedding in Cana (Khirbet Qana), expressing anger as he did in reaction to Peter not understanding key points he made, and crying at the death of Lazarus.

How did the strengths and weaknesses of these Jewish communities inform and then buttress Jesus's mission and the sheer knowledge and required energy to put them as context and content before his fishermen, other disciples, and circles beyond them? This question merits our attention, for we need to know its nature, consistency, and distinctions with what had preceded him in Judaism.

We know that Jesus was a teacher who gained his listeners' respect appropriate to that of a rabbi. He knew and taught the centrality in Judaism of the Law of Moses and the words of the prophets. He taught as the occasion required: one on one, often in the quieter moments of his days and nights, to groups gathered for discussion and reflection, and to extraordinarily large crowds, each setting to reach with his message those surrounding him in their present in order to focus their present on their inescapable future of death and judgment. We find it at Matthew 22:37–39: "Love the Lord your God with all your heart and with all your soul and with all your mind. This is the first and greatest commandment. And the second is like it: Love your neighbor as yourself. All the Law and the Prophets hang on these two commandments."

As to the centrality of the Ten Commandments, the first commandment is of profound importance, the first three summarize a person's relationship with God by teaching us to both love and fear God, the following seven teaching us to love within our family and among our neighbors, meaning others. Jesus knew thoroughly the Law of Moses as its essence sought both harmony between God and a person and harmony between persons. His teachings were not intended to empower the people in a taking of authority by force from Roman governors and temple priests. Rather, his teaching arose from his knowledge of what the law was meant to accomplish and each person's duties in respect to themselves and others. They were meant to set in our minds a deeper understanding of why wrong is wrong by more fully understanding their detrimental consequences for self and others. Despite the Law and its permeation in Hebrew lives, generations increasingly further away in time from that covenants' origins resented both its imposition of stringent restrictions on their personal conduct and the consequences of their failure to heed them.

Jesus's commandment to love one another, within and beyond family, was not new, for it was found in the Jewish Bible, but his emphases gave heightened intensity to it. Over centuries it transitioned to a Christian culture in which a core tenet was to care for others without requiring equivalency. Caring for self may be a firm basis for caring for others, but it must lead to that care without a requirement or even expectation of reciprocity. Jesus knew that one's own negative attitudes most often fostered negative attitudes among others, wrongfulness engendering further wrongfulness, in short, hatred fed hatred and hate cast a broad and deep negative focus in thought, conduct, and consequence.

A frame of mind deep enough to achieve a state of abiding love of others arises from an awareness of God's deep love for us all and a desire to reflect God's love through one's relationships with others. Additional elements of or gateways to this love are respect, endearment, appreciation, forgiveness, and patience, each and together sufficient to motivate the caring of others, a mind-opening mental doorway being kindness, as in be kind to one another. What is set out in his reading in the three instances—at the Nazareth synagogue, in the Beatitudes, and in Matthew 25—are examples of his intentions, but they also set out what he expects from those who should reflect God's love for humanity through love of individuals within it. Together they are descriptions of his ministry's intended focuses on those persons in the greatest of human needs.

Does this commandment, requirement, direction, and insistence to love one another reach a level to which a person can be held accountable at his judgment? It does. How? If God not only loves a person but expects him to love others and he does not, that person has made a decision, taken an action, contrary to God's commandment, a dangerous place to be in relation to God.

Attitudes based on the centrality of Jesus's descriptions of loving one another made honoring the commandments more attainable by reducing both the number and the victimization of those who suffered. As there was an intended mutuality in God's love for a person and a person's love of God, there were mutualities among all the commandments. Speaking in our days' terms, offspring honoring parents ought to generate more honoring of the offspring by their parents. Not committing adultery and not being inclined to commit it is a far stronger basis for mutual trust than a wedding altar's too-often rote pledge of faithfulness. The reverse of that further proves the point, for loss of trust particularly as to that commandment can seldom ever be completely re-established if not by total forgiveness.

Abiding by what was written on the stone tablets would be more aligned with what God had intended, bringing day-to-day life on Earth closer to the ideal. Though this changed world would not become a heaven on Earth, it would be a place closer to our expectations of it in personal and familial, social and cultural, clan and tribal, and ultimately in national, religious, and civilizational senses than the often-seeming hell on Earth. Envy and the jealousy which arise from transgressions, anger and the outrage which arise from them, lying, and murder and theft and the abuses of persons which arise from them would abate, and a larger peace in the public space would be a consequence of the internalized peace of the many, occasionally becoming in time a habit.

Jesus had multiple facets of his personhood, but he was neither naive nor uninformed The commandments' unmistakable clarity, set out by the God who had chosen them as his people, had had limited impacts within the affairs of Jewish humanity in the fifteen centuries following Moses's descent from the mountaintop. Jesus knew that observant Jews had adhered in the main to these dictates, but he knew also that those lives and that faith had existed geographically inside of successive foreign occupations, each occupier the dominant power and professing alternative religious faiths. He knew his own demonstrations of godly powers would bring greater attention to his substantive messages on the consequences of living and not living in accordance with them. He knew his attempt needed something more than the ten in order to assure wider success in following them. If you truly loved others, abiding by the commandments would be easier, perhaps far easier. He sought to change what was seen by some Jews as God's imposition of the commandments to a renewed and positive attitude toward them, one nurtured by love and individual and joint searches for validation.

The beginning of Jesus's public ministry is highlighted by an event in Nazareth which received immediate and profoundly dramatic attention. It was a particular reading by him, most probably at the synagogue, though the place is irrelevant to the magnitude of what he did. The traditional form of a worship service was prayers and two readings, one from the Torah (*Nevl'im*) and one from the Prophets, such readings known in Hebrew as *Haphtar-ah*, sometimes their consecutive reading followed in Aramaic, and then a sermon. In this instance, he read from the sixth-century BC prophet Isaiah:

> The Spirit of the Sovereign Lord is on me, because the Lord has anointed me to proclaim good news to the poor. He has sent me to bind up the broken-hearted, to proclaim freedom for the captives and release from darkness for the prisoners, to proclaim the year of the Lord's favor.

Then he rolled up the scroll, handed it to someone and sat down and, knowing that this passage embodied the long-sought hopes of his Davidic kinsmen for the reinvigoration of Israel, he added: "Today this scripture is fulfilled in your hearing." Yet he had stopped his reading precisely before Isaiah's next line on the "day of vengeance of our God" to make it unmistakably clear at this outset that he had not come as a militarily inclined messiah to rid Israel of its Roman oppressors, but to redeem mankind in a far more important and wider sense than that narrowness and, to underscore that, he was prepared for this mission.

Author Jean-Pierre Isbouts articulates that distinction: Jesus knew that his role was not to be that of a warrior-king but that of a spiritual leader regardless of risks to him, and this well-timed dramatic reading conveyed that distinction and began those risks. The dramatic change in message set out is why it was not readily accepted by even his neighbors. They believed the messiah would mirror the military, political and governmental leadership of King David, a combination which as the centuries passed had failed to protect ancient Israel from invaders and occupiers. In contrast to his own ancestor, David, Jesus offered a messiahship of love, it reflecting God's love of humankind and the need for love of one another. Jesus's sword was to be one of thoughts, words, and their actions.

It is essential to our knowledge of Jesus to understand this event's fundamental moment for Jews, for even youngsters early in their learning of the law and the prophets were familiar with the words he read. Its uniqueness arises from Jesus's continued words that this reading *fulfilled* Isaiah's prophecy, albeit not a single of these words implied the political-military leadership which they had long sought and expected. Those listening could have regarded his words as a straight-forward declaration that he was committing his life's work to its words' focuses: bringing good news to the afflicted, healing the broken-hearted, proclaiming liberty to captives, opening prisons to those who were bound, and proclaiming the year of the Lord's favor, taken together a commitment to do good, a life choice intention shared with family and neighbors. Yet, these words were so identified with the messiah sought by them, they could not be separated from that connection, especially after his claim of fulfillment. These moments changed histories: Judaism's and the world's.

Initially, those there spoke well of him and his words, but then the atmosphere changed. A tense conversation must have arisen between those who heard his reading and then between them and him. Some were angered, rising up and pushing him down the streets toward the mile-and-a-half distant brow of a high hill, presumably intending to cast him to death or great injury. Where they probably went, a pilgrim can still go.

While there is no assurance that it is the exact place, although there are no others within their walking distance which fit the scriptural description, it is the place of "the Lord's Leap" (*Saltus Domini*), also known as the Mountain of the Leap (*Jebel el-Kafsah*), Mount Kedumim, and more topographically Mount Precipice. Once there or elsewhere, they paused, perhaps because they took note that he was their neighbor Joseph's son or they had begun to ponder in the intervening moments and discussion with one another what he had said and what it might mean or both of these considerations. Scripture informs us they desisted, and he passed through them and went his own way.

His ministry was now underway, and his and our world would never be the same. Inasmuch as these words from Isaiah were at the core of his mission and inasmuch as Jews anticipating a new messiah knew them well in that context, it is a near certainty that he quoted or alluded to them on other occasions, including especially at initial meetings with his disciples and other followers.

Many in Nazareth lacked belief in him to an extent it later evoked from him one of the more recognized self-observations on his ministry, as stated in Mark 6:4: "A prophet is not without honor except in his own town, among his relatives and in his own home." But, as his kinsfolk persisted in efforts to maintain links to him, they became increasingly aware he was building a following in Galilee and Judaea, and in time they, too, responded to that recognition. Having first regarded him as overstepping his place among them, their kindred, and neighbors, they became amazed at the depth of his knowledge and public responses to his preaching, and they began to speak better of him.

In time, Jesus's followers were not of a singular opinion on what was occurring in the wake of his teaching. Nearly all thought their task was to strengthen Judaism by adhering to the Law and the prophets and to reduce the risks of assimilation of tenets and practices from other faiths, be they Greek, Roman, or otherwise.

Because many believed him to be the messiah, they believed he was Judaism's fulfillment, not an originator of a new sect to exist beside others.

As to the circumstances of this account, I have stood on what is believed by many to be the floor of an ancient synagogue in Nazareth. It may or may not be the one of Jesus's reading, but there is archaeological evidence that the floor of this reading survived because it was used as the floor of a Greek Uniat church from the year 1741, which is believed to have been built on the foundation of a school, it in turn having been built on the foundation of a synagogue from biblical times, and Nazareth was not a large enough community to have two synagogues. Something else of significance happened to the synagogue between the time of Jesus and 1741. Following battles between Persians and Byzantines from 614 AD to 628 AD, Jews who had cast their lot with the losing Persians were expelled from the area. Muslim Arabs took possession of the abandoned synagogue and remodeled it into a mosque, while remaining Jewish Christians in the area may have converted to Eastern Orthodox Christianity.

The Gospels reveal Jesus's disappointments, deep ones, at rejections of his message from within his family, among his neighbors, and by others, but they were not unanticipated. They emanated from how he, his message, and his actions bore few parallels with the leadership of King David into whose lineage he was born, and around which expectations of a new messiah had persevered for centuries of Judaism. His disappointments included his disciples showing repeatedly that they did not understand either his messages or his expectations of them in respect to their own roles in the future fulfillment of those messages. Failing as they did to move beyond the mental block of their past and present, they often let personal fear undercut the strength required of them to fulfill his intensions of the future.

Jesus was well prepared to give answer to those that doubted. In response to Peter's exclamation that he was the Messiah, the son of the living God, he declared himself to be that fulfillment. His words to the disciples after his resurrection point to the necessity of their having extraordinary levels of personal courage in order for his mission to be heard by the old and new ears of Jews and Gentiles. I have at the intersection of Scripture and logic concluded that the accusatory voice of Jesus heard by Paul on the road to Damascus, occurring about a half-dozen years after Jesus's crucifixion and the turning over of his mission to his apostles, set into motion through Paul a necessary reinforcement of what was required, what was to be done and the personal courage among them and others to do it. Paul reinforced Peter because, once again, Peter needed it, and together they, others, and Jesus's message grew before and after Paul and Peter gave their lives in Rome as punishment for laying its foundations more broadly within Rome's empire.

CHAPTER 7

Jesus and John the Baptist

Understanding Jesus is amplified by what we know about his existential nature as captured at the first chapter of the Gospel of John:

> In the beginning was the Word, and the Word was with God, and the Word was God. He was with God in the beginning. Through him all things were made; without him nothing was made that has been made. In him was life, and that life was the light of all mankind. This light shone in the darkness, and the darkness have not overcome it.

This passage is set out twice in these pages because it is of foundational importance to understanding Jesus and his brief physical life on Earth between God's infinite past and their infinite future. That is fundamental to understanding Christianity. It is also a way of understanding John's understanding of Jesus and another John's, John the Baptist, role in the advent of Jesus's ministry. John's words declare the divine context for the only begotten son of God, and John the Baptist's words declare he has arrived.

Most know of John's and Jesus's respective baptisms and executions, but few grasp their additional relationships and their complexities. John was the son of Elizabeth, and Jesus was the son of Mary. Elizabeth's and Mary's pregnancies overlapped in part, John born six months earlier than Jesus. Given their mothers' kinship, John and Jesus were most probably first cousins or, less probably because of the age difference between Elizabeth and Mary, perhaps an aunt and a niece, therefore second cousins. In their means and ends, while John was full of truth, Jesus was full of truth and grace.

John and Jesus were both conceived, born, raised, educated, lived, preached, taught, and were executed as Jews. The intentionally mocking inscription INRI, an abbreviation for the Latin words *Iēsus Nazarēnus, Rēx Iūdaeōrum,* translated as "Jesus Nazarene, King of Jews," on carved wooden signage above Jesus at his crucifixion, captures prophecy, discernments of his Jewish nature, and his moral leadership role within that faith. What was intended by this INRI description to mock with scorn captured unwittingly a depiction of him felt by the Jews who aligned their thoughts with his as a reforming voice within their faith.

The significance of the naming of Jesus cannot be overlooked, for it was heaven sent in a foretelling of his role. Matthew and Luke inform us he was named the proper Hebrew name Yehoshua, in daily Aramaic Yeshua, meaning "YHWH is salvation" which is God is salvation, and sometimes depicted in translation without participles as Lord Saves. Is there a scriptural summation of that complexity? Yes, for Matthew informs us that an angel instructed Joseph to name him this because "he will save his people from their sins." In Christian instances, this is translated from Joshua into Greek as Jesus, but remaining known in Jewish circles as Joshua ben Josef, that is Joshua, son of Joseph. An alternative identification with his place of birth is, of course, Jesus of Nazareth and capturing in title his Messianic role, again without participle, as Jesus Christ, but with the participle, Jesus the Christ.

Matthew 1:22 informs us that Jesus is the Emmanuel in fulfillment of Isaiah's prophecy: "A voice of one calling: In the wilderness prepare the way for the Lord; make straight in the desert a highway for our God" of which John the Baptist's messianic amplification added "for the kingdom of heaven has come near." All of this in the face of opposition from the Sadducees and Pharisees.

John the Baptist appeared as an itinerant preacher in the fifteenth year of the reign of Tiberius, that being in August of 28 AD. His ministry preceded the emergence of Jesus's, but not long after John's began, he and Jesus intersected again, even though their familial relationship had begun much earlier. So much so that as each was within his mother's womb, the maturing fetus of John reported by Scripture to have leaped at the presence of the maturing fetus of Jesus in Mary on the occasion of a meeting of their mothers. Additional similarities include miraculous conceptions, each involving the same messenger's roles, in the first instance to John's father and in the second to Mary and then Joseph. Add to this their extended family ties and their later dissent from the ritualism of the Sadducees and Pharisees, belief in baptism as the washing away within a person's psyche of emotional burdens arising from the commission of wrongful acts, the centrality of service to the poor in their many definitions, fulfillments of prophecies and declarations of new ones, prospects in the afterlife as an inescapable outcome in part of the earthly life, and their executions at the hands of powerful personages within their faith and within the land's governance.

While sharing tenets of their Jewish faith and perceptions of dominant issues in it, both addressing Jews as individuals and collectively as within the Jewish nation, they nonetheless had differing strategies to convey their messages. That's an important distinction. The changes which John most sought addressed Judaism more in its nationhood, and those most sought by Jesus were more addressed to personhood, each knowing the one affects the other. John's was profoundly declaratory as to what lay ahead for the Jewish nation. He was not subtle. The destruction of the Second Temple can be seen as a fulfillment of the warnings of both John and Jesus. After the death of John and seemingly out of frustration in him not achieving measurable results from his preaching among Jews, Jesus began addressing wider audiences and shared with his disciples the importance of his changed opinion about to whom his message was addressed as Gentiles joined Jews in the audiences.

Jesus spoke of John as an "Elijah who is to come," a reference to the prophecy found in Malachi 4:5–6 at which a prediction of a "great and terrible day" of judgment of the Jewish nation is set out. While a number of judgments occurred between that prediction and John and Jesus's lives, the baptizer's predictions were repeated vehemently, widely, and irritatingly to officialdom. He was asked by a delegation of priests, "Are you Elijah?" as if he were a reincarnation, to which he responded "I am not" (John 1:21), but Matthew makes it clear that John's spiritual and prophetic lineages did flow from Elijah, and there is another key element in respect to Elijah. In Luke 1:16–17 Gabriel appeared to John's father, Zechariah, as the latter was offering incense at the temple, and informed him this unexpected son John "will turn many of the sons of Israel to the Lord their God" and John would go forth "in the spirit and power of Elijah." John would later learn from 2 Kings 2:8 that the primary location chosen by him for baptisms was where Elijah had parted its waters nine centuries earlier in order to walk across the stream bed with his successor prophet Elisha. John would also know this baptismal site was near where Elijah was believed to have ascended from nearby Elijah's Hill (Jabal Mar-Elias) in the chariot of fire set out centuries later within William Blake's "Jerusalem" stanza. Not far from the site's east bank is the elevated ridge we know from accounts of the aged life of Moses as Mount Nebo. John was demonstrably aware of the intersections of the books of the law and prophets with the topography surrounding him.

The Benedictine biblical scholar Fr. Bargil Pixner has written: "After Jesus had been baptized by John in the Jordan near Jericho and spent time with him in Bethany-Beyond-the-Jordan, he remained in the fellowship of the Baptist," after which Jesus began conversing with the Holy Spirit and baptizing with water near Aenon, an area of "abundant waters." A scriptural passage has Jesus leaving immediately after his baptism, but that might need a clarifying definition of immediacy, or have been from a particular encampment site but not from John's continued accessibility. His remaining with John could have been an irritation to some of John's followers, they not knowing what John and Jesus knew between themselves about their mutual and respective roles. Their conversations would have dealt with those roles and who else was there with John and from where they had come, an important element of Jesus accepting John's trust as to his own inner circle.

Matthew 4:12–14 tells us that Jesus returned to Galilee upon learning that John had been imprisoned by Herod Antipas, an observation implying longer than immediate, Jesus suspecting from this awareness that their once-shared roles would soon become his alone. John had said of their roles "He must become greater; I must become less." (John 3:30) Jesus's suspicion was fulfilled when Herod Antipas, driven by sexual desire, acceded at his birthday celebration banquet to the request of his step-daughter Salome, the wife of king Aristobulus of Chalcis and Asia Minor and mother of their three sons, to bring to her John the Baptist's head as a prerequisite for the fulfillment of his desire. Herod was reluctant because he knew of John's popularity, but John's admonishments of Herod, his wife Herodias and Salome as to each's wrongful life choices and Herod's fear of looking weak before his powerful guests were decisive. It is from Josephus's *Jewish Antiquities* that we get these details not set forth in Matthew or Mark, but Matthew concluded that the people of Galilee who had sat in darkness benefitted from "the great light" of Jesus's ministry in the wake of John's execution.

Jesus returned to Nazareth from which he moved to Capernaum to live with Peter and his wife's family, fulfilling the prophecy of Isaiah about Nazareth and Capernaum within Zebulon and Naphtali fulfilling the geographic origins of the long-awaited messiah. It was here that he first recruited four fishermen to his mission as he did the tax collector Levi, whom we know as Matthew.

Founded as a fishing village during pre-Roman Hasmonean rule of the region, its name, Kfar Naḥūm (כְּפַר נַחוּם in Hebrew), meaning Nahum's Village, existed because its location was the intersection of the major trade route of Via Maris. It became his own city, and Jesus's mother and his brethren in time joined him and his disciples there. Distant in geography and focus from the dominant cities of commanding influences in government and in faith, Capernaum was a community of about 1,500 inhabitants. While that number was ten times larger than Nazareth, it was ten times smaller than bustling Magdala. Capernaum's occupied a large territory, given that fishermen and others maintained fields for agriculture and husbandry.

When Capernaum was identified in 1838 by an American researcher of biblical sites, it appeared as little more than rubble, although he readily identified among its ruins what appeared as an ancient synagogue. By 1894 the Franciscans had purchased the site from Bedouins, and sophisticated archaeological work was undertaken by German, French, and Italian crews before it was interrupted by World War I, the resulting fall of the Ottoman Empire, and the 1920s rough-edged realignment of the borders of Middle Eastern states from that fall. After a delay of over forty years, Franciscan archeologists unearthed between 1968 and 1991 the center of Jesus's adopted hometown. What a hard-work find it was, for while Capernaum had no paved streets, only a few straight streets with many winding alleys, it consisted mostly of one-story residences of one to several rooms, the structures built around courtyards where craftsmen worked and children played. There were buildings, some built wholly of stratified limestone and others built with limestone on top of basalt bases. It was a community of olive presses, grindstones for various grains, facilities for the production of stoneware, and glassware and on its outskirts the tanning of hides.

Among Jesus's miracles, one in Capernaum stands out for its forecast of the rise of Christianity beyond its Jewish roots. Capernaum had a garrison of Roman soldiers under the command of a centurion, his title indicating he officered a hundred men, he and them serving the emperor in Rome through their stationed service to Herod Antipas. This is the centurion whose servant Jesus healed, but there is more to be known about this particular healing for its circumstances and consequences had a significant impact on Jesus. It is not known whether the garrison was built prior to these men's service or as one of their early tasks, but its ruins indicate better building than others in Capernaum, which probably illustrates it was not built by towns people. It was so sophisticated in its design and construction that it had a caldarium (a hot plunge bath), tepidarium (a room heated by underfloor heating), and frigidarium (a cool or cold plunge bath). The centurion had either personal means or access to other funds for he used them to build a synagogue for Jewish worshippers. That deserves an exclamation mark in Judaic and Roman histories. If the centurion used his own soldiers to build the synagogue, they were probably gathered from Phrygia, Gaul, and Germania which in our time is respectively western Turkey, France, and Germany. Archaeologists observe it was spectacular.

Scripture is clear that Jewish elders in Capernaum informed Jesus that this centurion loved the Jewish nation to such an extent he had built this synagogue for them, but that's not the end of this account. The centurion also knew enough about the social rules of the Jewish faith that it would be inappropriate for him to receive the Jewish teacher Jesus into his Gentile home where his servant was ill, explaining to Jesus from that awareness that Jesus could perform the requested healing from a distance. Jesus did, then exclaimed to those near him, "I tell you, I have not found such great faith even in Israel." (Luke 7:9)

That observation kindled Jesus's expansion of the intended audience of his message from Jews alone to Jews and Gentiles, from his faith alone to his faith and beyond. This appears to be the starting point of the collaborative roles of Jews and Gentiles in the building of what was to become early Christianity. The event warrants a discussion of Jesus's miracles for their plentiful commission demonstrated his God-like power to heal and resurrect. What Jesus was telling those around him then and us now in his miracles through healing is central, actually a core, to understanding his messages. They demonstrated without parallel his authenticity.

There is something else to hold in one's mind as to Roman centurions in the Jesus story. In addition to this centurion, we find a centurion at the foot of the cross on which Jesus has just died, he entering the historical record in his exhortation, "Surely he was the Son of God." Because he exclaims it immediately following Jesus's death, he has been referred to as "the first Christian," but others may have said this or something similar without the words being caught by a bystander. There is the remotest, yes remotest, possibility that the centurion in Capernaum had been detailed by his superiors, because of their knowing of his first-hand knowledge of Jesus, to the Jerusalem district for the days of Passover.

More than thirty specific miracles are described in the Gospels, but their number is less important than their natures and the number of persons healed by them, especially given John's mention of larger numbers of miracles than those set out in the Gospel's individual accounts. Though his is the shortest of the Gospels, Mark reports more miracles than other chroniclers, and John describes these phenomena as signs instead of as miracles. Why? At least four reasons: to illustrate that Jesus had God-like power, to demonstrate his love for those whose lives were transformed by them, to express love for humankind, and to bring persons closer to Jesus's teachings. As Peter Brown sets out in *The Other Rome*, Jesus "was the bridge between heaven and earth." In no way until his resurrection and their witnessing of it was this more proved to his questioning disciples than when Jesus calmed a stormy sea. Fearing that storm-driven wind and water would capsize their boat and they would perish, Jesus ended the storm by rebuking that wind and waves. While miracles they had witnessed were startling, none was comparable to this power to control sky and sea. In amazement, they exclaimed "Even the wind and the waves obey him!"

Because miracles demonstrated Jesus's God-like power, they reinforced with high drama his teachings and received widespread attention beyond what his words alone could attain in the short run. But there was also a downside. Former Archbishop of Canterbury William Temple points out how the performance of miracles worked in that short term against Jesus's intentions as to desired perceptions of his teachings: "He is endowed with supernatural power, and uses it for the works of love. But His miracles are a hindrance to His main purpose rather than a help, because they lead men to think of Him as a wonder-worker and excite in them a quite unspiritual interest and curiosity." Realizing this, Temple points out, Jesus bid those whom he healed "to be quiet about it but many, if not most, were not silent," and how could they be as the recipient of such dramatic changes in their lives, appearances, and conduct and, further, their healings were obvious to others. Why then did he continue them? Temple answers that: "He still heals for Love confronted with need must meet the need if it can." To that point and not surprising to the attentive observer, they evidenced in the physical world what he set forth in his reading at the Nazareth synagogue and in his Beatitudes as the intentions of his ministry. He aided those in need of miracles and their life-changing consequences. Over the stretch of them, from the transformation of ordinary water into quality wine to his own resurrection, they validated his divine authority to persons healed, those witnessing the events, others learning of them, and not least his often doubting disciples. The love which Jesus had for others is captured among Christians by the Latin word for love, *caritas*, the root word of charitable.

Other miracles were restoring sight to the blind and restoring combinations of sight, sound and speech to others; ending neurological disorders and the physiological disorder of edema; ending the twelve-year-long vaginal bleeding, probably from an obstetric fistula, of a woman, her access through a crowd moving in procession around Jesus indicating she was a Gentile because she was not known to be uncontrollably bleeding to the Jews surrounding Jesus; healing a paralytic man and a crippled woman; returning another man's withered hand to normalcy; curing of chronic and infectious leprosy; and reducing a dangerous fever by ending its underlying cause.

His first miracle had changed the physical property of a considerable volume of water into fine wine at a wedding. He multiplied on at least two occasions a few fish into a number large enough to feed thousands of men and accompanying women and children; he ended life-threatening weather; he defied gravity by walking on the surface of water; there was the huge draft of fish caught after a night of his disciples' empty nets; there was the fish caught with a coin in its mouth; and he moved an illness from men to swine and then destroyed the swine.

Four miracles were the even more astonishing raising of the dead: a widow's only son; the twelve-year old daughter of Jarius, a synagogue leader near the Sea of Galilee and possibly in Magdala; Lazarus, astonishingly for the four-day length since his death; and, most imbued with why he had come to Earth, his own resurrection on the third day.

Their nature and number attest to Jesus's powers, but there is a different form of miracle tied to his teachings, and it is at the core of the intentions underlying his ministry, yet it is often overlooked by readers, viewers, and listeners. Its incidence is far, far greater in number than the miracles which made physically deformed, infirmed, diseased men and women whole again. It is transformation from healing the *inside* of a person, their mental state. An example?

A major television news network has aired a segment several times on the seeking of hundreds of thousands of persons each year to be healed of their physical infirmities at Lourdes in the Pyrenees mountains on France's southern border with Spain. It is a site of healings which followed apparitions believed by three children who witnessed them to have been those of Mary, mother of Jesus. They began in 1858. As was reported in the segment, a panel of medical and other experts now exists to evaluate purported claims of healing, and seventy-two in its years have been determined to be healed by no cause other than a miracle. That is a small percentage, but it is small because it is not a complete account, an addition told by a wheelchair-assisted man with a palsy-like disease giving rise to an awareness of this additional nature of healings. Perhaps he was selected to be interviewed because he comes to Lourdes repeatedly, but his physically apparent disease has not changed in that time. Yet, he averred he had been cured, his miracle not on the outside for the world to see but on the inside for him to experience. While he came to Lourdes seeking an outside miracle, he was experiencing a miracle inside. He made that point, and he cannot be alone in it, perhaps a far greater number experiencing this type of Lourdes experience. It is wholly consistent with Jesus's teaching, his aspiration for each person, the peace which passes all understanding. Millions of persons come to that peace by accepting Jesus's teachings as the determinative guideposts in their lives. Each is a miracle touched by his message, not one requiring a touching of his hand or the hem of his garment.

The importance of the synagogue in Capernaum of the centurion's servant does not stand alone in an altogether other way. Archaeologist Michael Hesemann captured an intriguing connection of bread between birthplace, the Capernaum synagogue and the Eucharist. How so? Jesus, born in the village of Bethlehem (in Hebrew, "house of bread"), said in the synagogue in Capernaum that he would give himself as the bread of heaven so that those who ate of it might gain eternal life, set forth in John 6:35, 56 as "I am the bread of life. Whoever comes to me will never go hungry, and whoever believes in me will never be thirsty." This first declaration of the Eucharist was here in Capernaum, attested to in John 6:59 with "He said this while teaching in the synagogue in Capernaum."

Hesemann's *Jesus of Nazareth* evokes striking images of Capernaum, and they include the succession of its synagogues. When archaeologists first sought the Roman centurion-built synagogue, they could not locate it, but professional toilers among ruins learn lessons from the past which enable their present. One such lesson is recognition that builders often build anew on prior sites for reasons of containing costs by reusing readily available construction materials as well as historic (location) and religious (consecration) reasons.

There stood out an impressive fourth-century synagogue, known widely as the two-storied White Synagogue of Capernaum, built with white limestone quarried at some distance. The archaeologists undertook careful excavation of its ruins in remarkably good condition given the region's earthquakes, often brutal climatic conditions, and centuries of plunder by successive populations in need of stones quarried, transported, squared, or rounded by the labors of others. While not a conclusion shared by all, although the logic that no other synagogue ruins had been found reinforced it, they believed the White Synagogue was built on the centurion synagogue's footprint. Examinations of its many details confirmed it contained remnants of a prior synagogue which its rebuilders preserved as features of the successor one.

The discovery in the ruins of a cache of 30,000 Roman coins verified its linkage in historic time, and its magnificence demonstrated it was built at great cost. Hesemann reports the expense was most probably borne by the fourth-century Roman Emperor Theodosius I ("gift of God") who may have intended it as a physical "symbol of reconciliation between Jews, Jewish Christians and Gentile Christians" then living in the area. It is now regarded as the most impressive ancient synagogue in the territory of modern Israel.

There is a similar authentication of these lessons less than a minute's walk from this synagogue, and it is a restored and enlarged church built over an original church, itself built over the site of Peter's home in which Jesus and his family had lived.

The Franciscan Order's Pilgrimage Church of St. Peter in Capernaum stands impressively with a glass floor over the ruins of an octagonal church built over 1,500 years ago. It was a surprising archaeological find, for octagonal architecture was inconsistent with the ninety-degree corners of that era. Hesemann reports what was more surprising was it consisted of three concentric octagons, the widest with a diameter of eighty-two feet and the inner-most at twenty-three feet. When excavating around this site in 1968 in order to build a protective structure above it, archeologists discovered the church had been built over the remains of a house built following the beginning of the Roman period in 63 BC. That awareness confirmed the house had been transformed by renovation as early as the middle of the first century into a public meeting place from which it grew in only a few decades after the crucifixions of Jesus in Jerusalem and Peter in Rome into what Hesemann aptly describes as a sacred space, that is, a house of worship. Why this recognition through architecture? Because it was Peter's family house in which Jesus, Peter, and his brother Andrew had lived with their families. Other early Christian churches in the region were also built over sites regarded as holy, for the houses of men such as Peter and women such as Mary Magdalene sheltered persons on their respective physical and spiritual journeys.

An early Western European Christian pilgrim to the area, Egeria, noted as early as 383 AD in her *Itinerarium Egeriae* that "the prince of the apostles" home had been made into a church, a point noted in *National Geographic*'s December 2017 cover story "The Real Jesus" by Kristin Romey, that by the time Christianity had become in the fourth century the official religion of the Roman Empire, Peter's house had been converted into a house of worship. Its size was slightly larger than most houses in the immediate neighborhood, perhaps a response to the need to accommodate additional persons on special occasions.

Lest it be overlooked, Hesemann reports the Franciscans' Custody of the Holy Land, a custodial priory founded by Francis of Assisi as the Province of the Holy Land in 1217 and formally recognized in 1342 as one of only two Roman Catholic custodians of Holy Land properties, authenticated the house of the first Roman Catholic pope, the first Holy Father, that being Peter, and caused it to be preserved by successive restorations. Those attending the earliest services there were its first congregations. Yet, it was persons toiling in their respective lives who had lived in it, its rear courtyard containing an oven of sufficient size to prepare food for a large family and guests and its front court's soil concealing such everyday objects as bronze fish hooks.

Capernaum had a tax collector whose services included the assuring of the public order generally and, as it relates to this account, the accurate counting of fish caught in the lake narrowly, those fish regarded as property of the sovereign in order to justify the collection of multiple taxes on them in a succession from capture to plate. It stands to reason that the customs house was situated near the major Via Maris route of commercial trade leading to and from Mediterranean ports. Because no town of consequence lay on the nearby Jordan River, Capernaum had become the border town between Herold Antipas's Galilee and his brother Philip's Tetrarchy. There is more to be experienced in this village scape of building blocks crumbled by earthquakes, weather, and time. It is being physically, and emotionally, surrounded by stones in place when Jesus walked among them and weighed the intricacies of his ministry and its relevance to his neighbors.

It was here particularly that Jesus gathered and taught. It was from here that he would travel and to which he would return. In his preceding walk from Nazareth, to which he had returned following his baptism, to Capernaum, he had traversed Wadi Hamam (Pigeon Valley) and come to Heptapegon, a fishing ground for Capernaum fishermen, whose name means Seven Springs, a word which the Arab population was to reconfigure as Tabgha. Although Tabgha was a small area in land size, it was to become a place of major importance in the emergence of what became Christianity, for it was the site of an expression of foreboding knowledge given from Jesus to Peter which Jesus understood far more than did Peter. We will return to it. In the late 1800s the then malaria-infested Tabgha was acquired through the tenacity of German spiritualists and Italian priests for its scriptural importance from Bedouin and Turkish landowners and redeveloped as a community with a pilgrimage hostel and adjacent farmlands, the hostel expanded in recent years into a modern and comfortable facility. Tabgha came much later in Jesus's life than the young age at which we note his own awareness of that life. What of these crucial points?

Jesus said in Jerusalem at the age of twelve and in the presence of his parents and assembled rabbis that he was committed to being about his father's work. This was most probably at Passover (*Pesach*), one of the three annual festivals during which all of the Jewish population was required to make pilgrimage to the temple, Passover in commemoration of the liberation of the Israelites from their slavery in Egypt. Jewish law required all children to be presented at the temple on the Passover preceding their thirteenth birthday. The circumstances of this conversation make it clear that Jesus was referring to his heavenly father's work, for he might have otherwise followed totally in the course of his earthly father's building trade. In the progression of his life from twelve to thirty, he was doing either one thing only or a combination of things, far more likely the latter because that is the nature of a life's experiences. While working with his father and others in many matters, his study of Judaism was central to his life. These eighteen years between twelve and the commencement of his ministry were not short in length for they encompassed around 200 months, and, at their end, his encounters with John the Baptist.

Jesus and John the Baptist's knowledge of their shared faith was drawn from the Pentateuch, the first five books of the Hebrew Bible: Genesis, Exodus, Leviticus, Numbers, and Deuteronomy, as well as the books of the Prophets (Nevi'im) and the concluding grouping known as the Writings (Ketuvim) which followed. The content of the first five is ascribed to recitations from Moses and was carried orally by group chanting for a hundred generations before being reduced to writing from the ninth to the fifth centuries BC. This word-by-word oral text was authenticated repeatedly by the process of many persons listening to each recitation so a misstatement would be corrected at once by those hearing it. There followed nineteen additional books of the Hebrew Bible, the twenty-four total known as the Written Torah, meaning written teaching.

There is more to the scriptural breadth of Judaism than this Written Torah, and it includes the Oral Torah which followed in time and was derived from other ancient texts and writings, the Written and the Oral serving as the bases for law and moral obligations. They encompass how, as a people, Jews were given an identity by god with a covenant intent on binding them to those moral obligations. This context for Jewish Scripture may be a reason among others for why words matter intently in Judaism, the Torah's beginning with "Let there be" introducing the countless thousands of words which follow, the people of the Torah knowing that it is a combination of words which constitutes the narrative.

The interpretation which overarched both written and oral texts is known as *Midrash*. In the seventeen centuries between Moses and Jesus, divisions of beliefs, articulated by rabbis and heard by congregations adhering to them, had occurred. Jesus's teaching was a composite of his beliefs and their direction which, if they had remained internal to Judaism, could have reformed it in ways thought then to be so fundamental they were not accepted.

While Christianity in largest measure emerged from Judaism, it was so distinct in how adherents were to interact with one other, in time it was not seen by most Jews and early Christians as a radically reformed Judaism, rather as a new religious faith originating from it. It survived and grew as that. While it is easy to short-hand in thought that the Christian's Old Testament is the same as the Hebrew Bible, that's wrongly thought for, while it mostly is, it is not exactly either in content or translations from Hebrew to Greek to modern languages, some alleged to have slants intended to accommodate Christian fulfillment of its prophecies. This neither reduces Christians' respect for the Hebrew Bible as mostly their Old Testament nor the fact of the unity of the Old and the New in the Christian Bible for, as "archaeologist, author, screenwriter, director, and producer of works addressing various historical periods, particularly the time period of Jesus" Professor Jean-Pierre Isbouts has pointed out: "No other book has been of greater influence on the development of Western civilization than the Bible. It is the foundational text of Judaism and Christianity and accepted as divinely inspired scripture by Islam."

During the years in which Jesus lived the Jewish faith within him and expressed it to others, there were deepening differences in tenets and practices between its two dominant branches and two sects, four expressions altogether. Each had its opinion about how the fundamental laws of ancient Israel should be followed in Jews' daily lives. The Sadducees (*Tzedoqim* in Hebrew, literally "acts with kindness towards God and creation") and the Pharisees (*Perushim,* meaning "separated ones") were those two branches, and they dominated Jewish religious power and practice in Jerusalem. That separation seems a break away from what was the dominant Judaic power structure at the time of the naming, the Sadducees, a dissent deep enough to have generated their naming. Jerusalem itself was a political, religious and commercial city in which order was assured and stability maintained through a complexity of authorities of and compromises between governors, military leaders, high priests and merchants. What the Pharisee and Sadducee high priests did agree on was their opposition to any Jewish religious expression other than their own, an animosity which constituted a substantial threat to Jesus and the content of his different message to the Jewish nation.

The Sadducees did not accept with equal authority the Oral Torah, insisting the Written Torah was clear in its text and needed no elaboration. In respect to a key teaching of Jesus and advocacy of others, Sadducees rejected the immortality of the soul, a consciousness which survives physical death, and thereby the possibility of resurrection, primarily because those concepts were not found in the Written Torah, Judaism's foundational text. It is not a simple digression to inquire as to whether the existence of a life form as demonstrated by Moses's encounter on the mountain top at which he received commandments for rightful living further opened the intellectual window to a realm in which souls survive the bodies' earthly deaths, a soul's future existence and its nature determined by assessment of its earthly life as measured by the commandments laid out by that form. I refer to "further opened" because preceding religiously-based cultures, such as the Egyptian and Mesoamericans, believed they had extraterrestrial origins and/or encounters.

The Sadducees consisted of a multilayered priest-based aristocracy and embodied a ritually focused life, including animal sacrifices from doves and pigeons to sheep and bullocks, each animal acquired by a penitent or a thanksgiver for the purpose of its sacrifice. Substantial incomes to the Temple and through it to the priests were derived in large part from these practices. Thirty-three days after his birth and in fulfillment of a ritual prescribed by Leviticus 12, Jesus's parents offered a pair of turtledoves or pigeons for sacrifice in thankfulness for his birth, being exempted as poor from the biblical provision to sacrifice a first-year lamb. Jesus's overturning of the tables of the money changers, who were an integral part of this sacrificial practice by facilitating payment in temple currency for animals to be sacrificed, was an attack on that practice. Few actions of Jesus have been more wrongly characterized than this one, but the money changers were not commercial "bankers," not "businessmen" to use our era's terms, but were rather temple functionaries operating in physical space associated with worship and exchanging currencies at rates favorable to the temple and its priesthood at the expense of penitents. Neither the temple priesthoods, nor the centrality of animal sacrifice or the writings in which Sadducees beliefs were inscribed survived the Second Temple's destruction.

The Pharisees accepted the Law of Moses and, unlike the Sadducees, they accepted the books of the prophets following the Pentateuch. Like the Sadducees, Pharisee priests had knowledge, prominence and influence, and some had significant inherited wealth and/or personal wealth acquired through positions held and/or marriage, or both. They were strongest in Jerusalem but, unlike the Sadducees whose temple responsibilities confined them there, the Pharisees were also strong in Judea more widely and in Galilee. There, they hounded Jesus as he preached and performed miracles, asserting that they were faked, and tried to entrap him in front of congregations accepting his, rather than their, descriptions of the faith they shared but often in disagreement.

With a belief in what the Oral Torah could add to understandings of the Written Torah, some Pharisees were open to the concept of an afterlife, this concept found in differing articulations in cultures surrounding ancient Israel. It is important to understanding Christianity to recognize that Jesus was not the originator of the concept of an afterlife transported by a soul which survived earthly death, albeit he professed and, far more dramatically, manifested it by his own resurrection.

As a consequence of Alexander the Great's conquests as far east as the Indus valley, accompanying and occupying and returning Greeks were exposed to Eastern beliefs in which life and afterlife constituted a cycle through reincarnation, and they returned to Greece and its Hellenistic extensions in the Levant, including Galilee and Judea, with the concept of an afterlife in mind and on tongue, but they were not alone.

There was another influence in respect to life after death, and it came from the Egypt which had conquered, occupied and governed their land at times and enslaved the Hebrew people for centuries. A written accounting of the Egyptian concept has been known for millennia. This Egyptian guide to their afterlives was then and is now *The Book of the Dead* first compiled from around 1,550 BC, but its later expanded text both reaches back another thousand years and then forward to Roman times. It is not a singular treatise but rather a collection of texts written by Pharaonic priests, and modern texts of this book re-assemble their content in systematic ways to make it more understandable. Known originally as *Book of Coming Forth by Day* and *Book of Emerging Forth into the Light*, it encompassed widely varying components dealing with the afterlife: "You will go, you will return. You will sleep, you will rise.... Rise, for you will not perish. You have been called by your name. You have been resurrected." The name of the deceased, which was felt necessary to unify their individuality, was required for their continued existence and ensured they would recall their earthly name when they came into unearthly realms. There had been a transition period of judgment in which the unrighteous were slaughtered and the righteous were further enhanced toward a divine-like afterlife, the righteous having successfully passed a "42 negative confessions" examination as to whether they had committed specific sins. An awareness of this judgment was a warning of the importance of everyday morality not radically dissimilar in particulars and consequence from the Law of Moses known to both Pharisaic Jews and later Christians. Raymond Faulkner, an English philologist of ancient Egyptian texts and editor of the *Journal of Egyptian Archaeology*, credited nineteenth-century American philanthropist Ogden Goelet for the conclusion in respect to those Negative Confessions that "without an exemplary and moral existence, there was no hope for a successful afterlife."

The Egyptian connection to the Hebrews dates at least from the Late Bronze Age, and it warrants an explanation. "Land of the nomads of YHWH" has been found among hieroglyphic inscriptions at a temple pillar and two New Kingdom Egyptian temples in what is now Sudan to modern Egypt's south. They are the earliest texts yet to be discovered that bear the name YHWH, the vowel-less form of Yahweh, the name of the Hebrew one god. They date from 1,400 BC to 1,300 BC and, as Titus Kennedy has set forth in his *Unearthing the Bible*, "the Egyptians of the 18th Dynasty and the pharaoh himself were familiar with the Israelites and the God they worshipped, suggesting contact and dialogue [before and] around the time of Moses, the Exodus, and the Hebrews wandering of the 15th century BC" and, as he points out elsewhere in its pages, additional hieroglyphics depict slaves as the molders of mud and straw bricks long recalled as compelled tasks of Hebrew slaves. A monumental stone inscription, erected originally at the island city of Elephantine near Aswan in Upper Egypt, records the military campaign of Amenhotep II, to Canaan from which he returned with over a hundred thousand captives to be used as slaves, a possible or probable massive exaggeration of number or their purpose. Once again, archaeology confirmed that which had been speculation or even denied when the 1993 discovery of an Achaemen Victory stele in ancient Dan confirmed David was known even by his neighbor kingdom in the ninth century BC to have been the king of Israel, the first of the Davidic dynasty. This kinghood was further confirmed by the Mesha Stele (also known as the Moabite Stone) of about 835 BC which references at its line thirty-one the "house of David."

With these points in mind, we return to John 1:1. An atheist may exclaim, "Look at the universe and its galaxies' billions of stars and tell me where among them is this heaven?" to which the Gospel of John responds "Everywhere!" even though heaven is a dimension which should not be confused in concept by arguments requiring consideration of it to be based solely on a known physical geography. It is as current a question now as it was when John reduced his answer to a writing. Despite declaring for many years that Earth's hominids cannot be the only intelligent life form in that vast universe, the once prevalent ardor for confirmation of unidentified flying objects by whatever description or reference and their inhabitants has cooled recently as some now fear that we not being alone in the universe adds weight to John's articulation. They may fear that confirming additional intelligent life will buttress, not denigrate, faith, especially if the nature of that life is identical or similar in physical and/or spiritual form to us, reflected scripturally by "God created man in his own image, in the image of God created them" (Genesis 1:27). This answer poses another quandary, for while such intelligent life forms elsewhere would further confirm John, as well as the Old Testament's Ezekial passages. There is no way, at least now, for a factual resolution of these questions, although an affirmative one someday will make for quite an experience.

There are two key definitional conceptions of the word heaven, one essentially in science in reference to the physical universe and the other essentially in religion in reference to the location of those with afterlives. There are differences in thought between the realms of astrophysics and those of spirit as to these heavens' origins, existences and futures, but there is no requirement of the deciding between the differences other than personal or systemic belief.

There are the heavens as a collective expression of the physical universe of stars and planets, galaxies and nebulae, comets, meteors and asteroids, black holes, and much else either in or beyond our own solar system as a part of it. There are also the heavens as a shared realm of afterlife consciousness, the dwelling place of souls however unknown to us its nature may be, which is the limitation of our own knowledge, not of God's capacity. A scientist and a theologian, making this distinction, can believe in the existence of both realms, but the cultural trend line seems now increasingly against it. The questions embodied in and answers derived from this focus are not knew; they are not solely a modern phenomenon. We know them among the differences of thought between

Sadducees, Pharisees, and later Christians, and they arose in intensity during the time of Jesus as a focus on the afterlife and life experiences for achieving or failing in its evaluation. If a person lived a life in total obedience to the Law of Moses, those touched in whatever degree by that exemplary conduct might more likely have comparable lives, together bettering themselves, family, neighbors and others. But the Sadducees did not believe in an afterlife, that the life lived here was the totality of a life, there being no physical or spiritual place to which a person's soul would go upon death of the physical body. If a person did not live their life respectful of God, parents and others, living in disregard of that Law, there were the enforcements of the eye-for-an-eye credo applicable primarily to physical harms, but what about other offenses and with what remedies to address them? Disrespect or denial of God? Respect God. Disrespect of the Sabbath. Respect it. Theft? Return the stolen item or pay its replacement value to the owner and learn from that experience. Coveting? Envying? Stop them, and accept what you have, work for more especially if it helps others, but not to strengthen your lot solely for comparative purposes. Adultery? Don't do it and, if you have, never do it again, for even the most committed acts of contrition and obedience can seldom if ever reestablish the marriage trust broken by it.

Without intending to be so, for they did not know what would follow in the wake of Jesus's ministry, the Pharisees unwittingly became a bridge in some ways between Judaism and Christianity. Behind his back and in his presence, they objected to and rejected him, and Jesus responded by avoidance when possible and by answer when confronted. The Sadducees accused the Pharisees of bringing other religions' beliefs, even their holy days, into Judaism, including that the Pharisees believed an afterlife of the soul was at least possible. In seeking to understand the differences of opinion among the Pharisees, we look to Nicodemus and later Paul.

What we know from Scripture informs us of Nicodemus' three occasions at Jesus's side. He first came to Jesus secretly, that setting and the probable content of his observations a warning to Jesus that the greatest risk to him and his teachings, even his life, was their threat to the Sadducee and Pharisee leaders and their dominating narratives. We see him again in several instances only two days apart. The first was his procedural-appearing defense of Jesus in his insistence the Sanhedrin, of which he was a member, hear Jesus in his own defense before it pronounced judgment of him. As to the Jewish priests' hostile actions, we cannot lose sight of the street value to them that they were able to accomplish the execution of Jesus, a successful exercise of limited authority within Rome's unlimited authority. We see him last in his bringing of a large quantity of expensive ointments for preparation of Jesus's body for entombment.

Jesus's trial before the Sanhedrin occurred as a consequence of what happened and did not happen at his trial before the Roman governor. Romans knew their own history, and they knew other experiences in this land too. Its governor, Pontius Pilate, would have recognized the similarities between Rome's ruling and administrative classes and Jerusalem's and maneuvered the tensions, when he could, to Rome's advantages. He feared being out of favor with Tiberius and those closest to him, and that limited the width of how to respond to the Jesus threat.

The intersection of that risk was not simple in its unfolding in the instance of Jesus. In that Pilate most probably did not speak fluent Hebrew or Aramaic and that Jesus did not speak Latin fluently, Pilate discussed with Jesus through an interpreter the charges brought against him by the priests whose authorities they felt threatened by his teachings. They feared not just the attention that Jesus was getting but more so the following he was attracting. Jesus's declaration, "My kingdom is not of this world. If it were, my servants would fight to prevent my arrest by the Jewish leaders. But now my kingdom is from another place" was an unambiguous summation before Pilate that Jesus did not regard himself as a threat to either Rome or the personage of Pilate and therefore Pilate should feel the same way. Given in response to Pilate's query "Are you the king of the Jews?" that Jesus replied, "You say that I am king" that emphasis on "You" was to make it clear that it had not been said by him but rather by the leadership of "the Jewish leaders." As we know from the discussion in John 18:33–38, Pilate responded to the priests with the powerful authority of his position "I find no basis for a charge against him." The dominant power of Rome had thereby spoken.

Jesus was condemned because the priest-assembled rabble cried aloud what they knew those priests wanted them to exclaim. Any leader who assembles a crowd for such a purpose knows how to manipulate that crowd, and it knows what to do when it is expected. They did it here, and the leadership is responsible for the result, protecting their own ties to the politically powerful at the capital expense of Jesus. Jews outside this event were increasingly supporting Jesus, and that support was what was unnerving Jewish officials protecting their own interests and positions of authority. This series of events occurred as a fulfillment of prophecy and was an affirmation of the most consequential reason Jesus came to Earth: To save humanity from sin, to forgive continued sin, and to redeem souls through grace for their failure. His death on the cross was set into motion from his miraculous conception, after which he was resurrected as proof of his divinity and return to from whence he came. These events demonstrate among additional reasons the absurdity of anti-Semitism.

Despite these realities, Pilate understood that if he released Jesus, he could be seen nonetheless by the powerful in Rome as taking unnecessary risks, therefrom that he was no friend of the Caesar, a disfavor endangering his position if not his life. This would have weighed heavily on him, and the priests knew that.

While we know as readers and viewers of Jesus's agonies on the day of his execution, no one will ever know it in the manner Jesus did. Nonetheless, each of us owes the deepest of gratitude to Jordan Peterson, the Canadian psychologist, author, and media commentator, for his capturing in words what Jesus experienced. He has set out a fullness of Jesus's awarenesses during his trial and crucifixion unparalleled in other writings:

> You cannot write a more tragic story; it's impossible. Why? Because it's the story of the aggregation of everything that people are afraid of.
>
> There is no death more painful than crucifixion, that's why the Romans invented it, it's a slow and agonizing death by suffocation essentially, dehydration and exposure; it's extraordinarily painful.
>
> Plus, you know it's coming, that's part of the story.
>
> Plus, your best friend betrayed you into it.
>
> Plus, your people turned against you.
>
> Plus, they're led by a tyrant who doubts truth.
>
> Plus, you're a victim of the Roman empire.
>
> Plus, you are completely innocent, plus everybody knows it.
>
> Plus, they choose a prisoner to be released from this experience instead of you, even though they know he's a criminal and they know you're innocent.
>
> And you're young, and you've done no wrong, and all you've done is to help people.

An AI-Generated Facial Image from the Shroud of Turin

Whether Pilate washed his hands in a bowl of water, and there is no scriptural account that he did, the practice was symbolic and common in Roman life to add drama to an exculpation of responsibility for an action of someone else's undertaking. At the end of his ten years as prefect, Pilate returned to Rome and entered into disputed history. His legacy as to Jesus fared best in the Ethiopian and Coptic Christian churches where, because of his reluctance to order the execution of Jesus, he is venerated as both martyr and saint. That he was not stoned to death for offense of Judaism, but rather executed on a Roman cross remains, in light of Pilate's finding of no reason, inexplicable to me.

Nicodemus the Pharisee came after the crucifixion with expensive ointments to assist Joseph of Arimathea and the women closest to Jesus in preparing his body for entombment. He would not have done these things had he not believed Jesus's teachings were important enough to be heard, to be considered, to be weighed.

What is there about Paul, another Pharisee, in these respects? His encounter with the accusatory voice of and temporarily blinding action of Jesus occurred six years later, not as soon as most would have believed absent that fact. I have wondered repeatedly what the eleven remaining disciples were doing during these six years. In the years which followed them, Paul changed the course of regional and then world history by co-nurturing with Peter, and them with others, the emergence of Christianity as a body of beliefs requiring increased structured organization to reinforce its growth. Nicodemus's association with Jesus was isolated, limited, and guarded as Paul's was sudden, at first inexplicable and continually risky but in short time committed and critically reinforcing of Peter in his, and then their, growing roles in spreading the Word.

Jesus's reference to the Pharisees as conceptually blind to what was occurring around them has an instructive connection to his later physical blinding of Saul on the road to Damascus and its, coincidentally or not, three days before his sight was restored after which his work in building early Christianity began. The Cambridge church scholar, Owen Chadwick of St. John's College highlights in his *The History of Christianity* this blinding as a truly profound moment in ushering in what would become Christianity: "The light on the Damascus Road...was beyond history and time, it came from eternity. But the humanity which it came upon was changing all the time and yet rooted in its past."

Paul was to become with Peter one of two cornerstones of leadership of a new faith as it moved from tenets among a voluntary association of believers to a structured organization of intended singularity and later a myriad of canons, synods and hierarchical and other denominations. The scholarly Paul was nearly the opposite of the Galilean Peter, the fisher and purveyor of netted fish.

Though born in Tarsus in what is now south-central Turkey, Paul was "born a Pharisee, of Pharisees," raised in Jerusalem and educated in its school of Gamaliel the Elder, who was a great-grandson of the renowned Jewish teacher Hillel. Acts 5 references Gamaliel as held in great esteem by Jews (Acts 22:3) and one who encouraged his fellow Pharisees to show leniency to Jesus's apostles (Acts 5:34-42) because if they were mere men nothing would come of their work and if they were men of God opposing them would be equivalent to opposing God. Despite his erudite education, Paul had chosen to be a worker of leathers, including tent making. In his devotion to the words of Jesus, he excelled unintentionally far beyond tents. Many Christian cathedrals' twin towers are in thanksgiving for and bear the names of Peter and Paul who, with the original apostles and others' expanded Christianity far beyond its origins. It was a process which encompassed several centuries as groupings identified with Jesus emerged, similar to Judaism but distinct nonetheless, they believing themselves, still as Jews, in what Jesus had left on Earth as a new sect within Judaism. In time Jesus concluded, and then shared with his disciples, that while he had come for the Jewish people he had later understood and he appreciated had come for Jews and Gentiles. His apostles were Jews, as Owen Chadwick has written, who "turned Judaism from a faith for the few into a faith for all," many of which were converted to it.

The books of the Bible which follow the Gospels are replete with accounts of the travels, sometimes with other disciples, such as Luke accompanying Paul, which spread the news of Jesus's teachings across a larger geographic face than the lands Jesus had known under foot. It was in Antioch on the Orontes River in what is now modern Turkey that the receptive response of Greeks to Jesus, his teachings and his divinity confirmed by miracles (Acts

11) led to the adoption of a new appellation for those who believed in him. It would be translated in time into the English language as Christians and Christianity, the followers of Jesus and the body of thought which housed his message and mission, and it continued to expand. Instead of Jesus, for there were many of that Greek name for the name Joshua in Hebrew, they chose the contextual descriptor of their Jesus, that being Christ, from the Greek word *christos,* the equivalent of messiah (משיח) in Hebrew, the anointed one of God, as their root word. He would be known as Jesus Christ, Jesus the Anointed, and as his followers took the appellation Christians, his detractors had little choice but to refer to them by it. Jesus had said it would be this way when he gave what is known as The Great Commission to his remaining eleven disciples. (Matthew 28:16-20) Some listeners to his message did not confess his thoughts because they had doubts, while others did not confess them for fear of persecution at a time it could be believed inwardly and lived outwardly by example of conduct but without public profession. Over the course of 2,000 years Christianity would continue to grow in many circumstances hidden under repressive theocratic and hostile governmental regimes. Today, it has more adherents than any other religious faith, which should speak loudly for itself.

As an attorney working internationally, I represented the Salesians Missions of Don Bosco, a welcomed matter widely known. Their founder, Father Giovanni Bosco, was formally recognized in 1934 as a saint. It is now a worldwide vocational order of the Roman Catholic Church, its priests specializing in spiritual advancement, known as formation, and job training of youth at which they excel. Baseball legend Joe DiMaggio and his brother Dom attended the Salesian high school in San Francisco. It was for me a life-changing experience, one which deepened my faith by seeing its impacts in peoples' lives. The order, headquartered in Italy, was asked circumspectly by representatives of the fervently declared atheist and communist government of China if its priests would assume responsibility for administration and education at certain trade schools in northern China, but this request came with restrictions. They could neither display crucifixes nor images of Jesus nor wear clerical attire. My reaction was: that could be a deal-breaker. The order's reaction? We will live our lives as Christians, and the students will come to see and appreciate that form of life. They would do it.

Saul had not taken the name Paul as a consequence of his conversion to what became Christianity though this is commonly and wrongly thought, for he already had Hebrew, Greek, and Latin names simultaneously, Saul being the Hebrew in his parents' recognition of the first king of united ancient Israel, Paulus in Latin and Paul in Greek, the latter carried into the first translation of Hebrew texts into Greek which were later translated into other European languages. It was primarily Paul who preserved in Christian worship many forms from Judaic worship. As Jewish prayer had ended with Amen, that meaning "so be it" and "truly," not having anything whatsoever to do with an appellation for male gender, so too did the Christian prayers which followed. To not fail to explain what another commonly exclaimed word means, "Hallelujah" consists of two joined, meaning "Let us praise together" and "God." Sacraments within the Christian church emerged over time, such as infant baptism to mark as Christ's own forever and the Eucharist, from the Greek *eucharistia*, meaning "thanks giving," a sacred meal declared by Jesus to be his body and blood, some believing it literally (transubstantiation) and others figuratively (representation).

Facilitated through his many travels to spread the good news, Paul's life means much to me. Knowing and appreciating James Cannon for years prior to, during and after publication of his *Apostle Paul* in which is a two-page map of Paul's travels, I began tightly encircling with a pen the names of the sites which I visited almost two millennia after Paul did, mine being Athens, Corinth, Damascus, Jerusalem, Joppa, Malta, Piraeus, Rome, Salamis, and Thessalonica, and I continue this focus on the enormous courage found in his missionary witness.

Jesus knew well the divisions within the Judaism of his time and what distinguished them from each other and other religious faiths. On the other hand, we need to know more about them to appreciate his understanding of them.

The Essenes were a small in number sect which emerged about two centuries before Jesus's life as an alternative to the Sadducees and the Pharisees. Essenes regarded those two dominant groups as "court Jews," an intentionally pejorative term to denounce Jews who had accommodated themselves to the successive authorities of Greek and Roman pagans while they strived nonetheless to be not wholly assimilated by Greeks and Romans. Some reasoned the Sadducees and Pharisees consented to be part of the Greek and then Roman systems in order to survive in that they had survived previous conquests.

The Essenes choose a radically different belief system, one featuring a monastic-like communal life, voluntary poverty and abstention from worldly pleasures, many practicing celibacy. We need to explore this more deeply than most would because there may be something here that has missed nearly all commentaries. Let's do that.

The Essenes adopted ritual bathing as one substitute for temple sacrifices and lived in accordance with a solar calendar of fifty-two weeks and 364 days that was not augmented by a leap year, as had the Temple calendar in its acceptance of what the Essenes felt were events derived from pagan worship. Most lived at distances from Jerusalem in order to avoid the corrupting influences of a big city. Their principal proximity to the Dead Sea Scrolls found at Qumran has given way to reference those scrolls as "the Essenes library," but that proximity fostered an inaccurate impression that they were confined to that area. They were not, and the Jewish philosopher Philo's writing set them in Galilee, Judea and what is now southern Syria. Some scholars believe Nazareth may have been influenced by Essenes, but they are not referenced by name in the New Testament, but they may have been indirectly at least once. At Mark 14:12, Jesus instructs his disciples to go into Jerusalem and there find "a man carrying a jar of water" to guide them to the place of the Last Supper. Mainstream Jewish men never carried water, for that was among immutable women's tasks, but Essene men did carry water. If the Last Supper was at an Essene's Jerusalem house, that raises the question as to what night of the week this event occurred because Essenes celebrated Passover a night earlier than Temple Jews. If true, this may answer long-unresolved questions as to the chronology of Jesus's days between Palm Sunday and his crucifixion.

John the Baptist's own reviling of the Sadducees and Pharisees and his life of severe self-discipline, poverty and ritualistic baptism were Essene-like. He might have been attracted early in his ministry to them but reasoned that their inward focuses denied him the proselytizing required to reach his intended large numbers. What was reflected by Jesus of the Essene's and John's messages? The eight intentions for the blessed in his reading in Nazareth from Isaiah and his Beatitudes come near. "The Spirit of the Sovereign Lord is on me, because the Lord has anointed me to proclaim good news to the poor" unmistakably points in that direction. They presage his words in Matthew 25:35–36: "For I was hungry and you gave me something to eat. I was thirsty and you gave me something to drink. I was a stranger and you invited me in, as I needed clothes and you clothed me. I was sick and you looked after me, I was in prison and you came to visit me."

Because of these humanitarian focuses, some modern-day activists proclaim Jesus was a socialist. It's an erroneous assertion because socialism, like capitalism, would not emerge as a coherent theorem until the 19th century. Socialism's compelled redistributions of property and income require heavy levels of taxation, which would have further worsened, rather than improved, the plights of the already-over taxed poor of ancient Israel. Furthermore, Jesus quite intentionally did not embody the messianic roles of political leadership necessary to propose, achieve and sustain such a dramatic change in the socio–politico–economic order and even further, his kingdom was not of this Earth. He was silent on the politics which encompass social policies, though he rightly detested corrupt elites.

Further removed in first century AD from the Sadducees, Pharisees and even the Essenes were the Zealots. They were a theocratic political movement which sought to incite Jews to rise in armed rebellion against Roman rule in order to compel its withdrawal. They believed this land belonged to God and could not therefor belong to an empire of political and military rulers. The Zealots functioned under veils of secrecy, the high risks of which led to their number being too few to challenge a Roman rule served by networks of informers and buttressed by well-trained military legions. They sought Jesus's support through influencing persons around him, a tactic which generated caution on his and his disciples' parts to avoid such identification in fact or appearance. Jesus and his disciples were apprehensive from the earliest days of his ministry about surveillance of them by Pharisees and Romans. If legend and history are compatible, their end as a sect came at Masada at their own decision to commit group suicide rather than yielding to death by the swords of Rome's fabled Tenth Legion founded by Augustus Caesar himself.

In the face of the Pharisees and Sadducees who had come to witness John's baptisms, he added:

> I baptize you with water for repentance. But after me comes one who is more powerful than I, whose sandals I am not worthy to carry. He will baptize you with the Holy Spirit and fire. His winnowing fork is in his hand, and he will clear his threshing floor, gathering his wheat into the barn, and burning up the chaff with unquenchable fire.

Upon hearing of John's baptizing, Jesus, his brethren, and perhaps others in Nazareth had traveled south to experience firsthand what John was undertaking at the Jordan. Upon John's recognition of Jesus in his presence, which recognition may indicate they had met previously, he insisted to Jesus: "I need to be baptized by you" for baptism was a washing away of sin and he knew Jesus to be without sin. Jesus rejected that conclusion and told him "Let it be so now, for thus it is fitting for us to fulfill all righteousness," upon which John baptized him. That all four Gospels give attention to Jesus and John spending time together illustrates its importance to Jesus's formation of his ministry and assessments of persons to be part of it. John's ministry began quickly to recede as Jesus's grew rapidly into wider public awareness.

Few biblical sites' locations were more elusive and for centuries than where John's baptizing of Jesus occurred. Described in John

1:28 as "took place in Bethany across the Jordan," the persistent efforts of historians, geographers, and archaeologists were expended to identify where it was within the physical realm of Perea, it being east and outside of Herod Antipas's and the Roman prefect of Judea's jurisdiction. They suspected a key clue would be the site of Byzantine Empress Helena's fourth-century constructed church, for it was reported in her time to be near the baptismal site. Where it and a successor fifth-century Byzantine church were remained less a mystery after 1994. The Israeli–Jordanian peace treaty of that year enabled the Jordanian army to clear landmines along Jordan's east bank, and archaeologists followed in the sometimes dust and sometimes mud with six years of excavations. Near the remains of a Roman period community of Jews was found the ruins of the church believed to be St. Helena's, succeeded in only a few centuries by one built by the Byzantine emperor Anastasius. It is near the river ford of Hajlah, not far from the Essene community near Qumran by the Dead Sea, perhaps adding some credibility to a possible relationship between John and the Essenes. Adding to the probability of this site as the authentic baptismal one, a Greek Orthodox church site from the fifth century was found on the Israeli, western side of the river.

While the Essenes' daily baptism was tied to earthly cleanliness, John's baptism was a sign of turning to God with a conscious desire for forgiveness for sin, an act intended to bolster an individual's spiritual transformation, for he had reasoned that daily baths as just bathing would not save sinners from divine judgment. While John chose to attack openly those in power and their lifestyles with words, until Jesus came near the end of his ministry, Jesus avoided those in power by maintaining distance from them. Luke informs us that as Jesus took his message increasingly to the people, acts which made the powerful in Jerusalem more aware of him, he too would then withdraw to this area east of the Jordan, from which he would return to Galilee. Archaeological evidence points to where John had lived for this brief time was not much more than an outpost of lodging for caravan drivers, a customs office, and huts for ferry operators, toll collectors and frontier guards.

Jesus formulated his initial mission around a shared goal with John: to save Jews from both the earthly and eternal consequences of living in disrespect of the commandments. His words made clear that he was teaching to fulfill the law expressed in the Pentateuch, and his life evoked reminders of prophecies set out in the Torah. With such a mission addressed to the lives of individuals as individuals, restrained from addressing the future of the Jewish nation as John the Baptist did, opposition to his mission and to him might have been minimized, but they were not. His commitment to unilateral forgiveness fundamentally challenged the bilateral practice of a proffer of forgiveness by one party and its acceptance or rejection by the second and all that would then occur. There were three levels of forgiveness in Judaism: *Selichah*, the offending person's act of seeking forgiveness; *Mechilah*, the offended person's wiping away of the offense; and *Kapparah*, the equalizing atonement accomplished, including especially at Yom Kippur. Jesus proposed that *Mechilah* be sufficient which would have altered the nature of atonement. In my lawyer's parlance, what Jesus set out was a unilateral act of forgiveness in place of the bilateral act of atonement. The consequence left Jews with their form of forgiveness and Jesus's followers then and later their form, both of which seem to me, as one of the latter, to be fine.

Further to this cluster of issues, Jesus's unequivocal declaration of the certainty of life after death was a direct challenge to the theology of the powerful Sadducees. Still further and in addition to animosity toward him in the religious realm, there were the

Roman and Herodian rulers and their ruling classes determined to suppress any destabilizing influences in the public sphere. The status quo which benefitted them was carefully managed, but it prevailed for only a few decades after Jesus's resurrection ushered in the gradual growth of a new community of faith.

Nearly forty years after John's and Jesus's deaths, what they predicted through warnings came to pass in startingly large measure. Jewish factions inside Jerusalem walls were so divided they could not agree on a shared and thereby strengthened defense and both burned the other's granaries resulting together in near starvation. Jewish and other inhabitants fell to the Roman sword, and its Second Temple, decades long in reconstruction, was looted and then destroyed as their temple, it quickly becoming a site in Roman thanksgiving to their pagan gods. Jews were killed, enslaved or exiled, only remnants surviving to begin regrowing in numbers wherever they lived. This catastrophe appears to have been the event prophesized by, and as to which John and Jesus had urged watchfulness and readiness by rightful living and repentance for wrongful living, but such a conclusion is better assessed by Jews, not those of other faiths.

Jesus's assurance, which the Sadducees opposed, that a person who lived their life in accordance with the commandments in their thoughts, words and deeds would pass to a subsequent life following their earthly death, gained enlarging numbers of adherents. It was a process through which a person was to have growing confidence reinforced by personal conduct until it became habitual, and nothing was to be, nothing now is, more demonstrably relevant to the prospects of their succession to an afterlife than his. Flavius Josephus wrote several decades following the deaths of John and Jesus that the Pharisees did believe the soul was immortal and those of good persons would pass into other mortal bodies, a reincarnation of sorts.

While the Pharisees in contrast to the Sadducees believed in the possibility of an afterlife, they probably believed the successive life would occur in a realm other than Earth, not as a consequence of resurrection in an early morning's stone tomb in Jerusalem a day and parts of the preceding and the following days (that's calculated as three days in Jewish reckoning) after an earthly death, as was the case with Jesus. There were resurrections already set out in the Hebrew Bible following the books of the Pentateuch but, even among the receptive Pharisees, it was more a theological postulation than an expectation of a near-term personal experience. There are in the Hebrew Bible several quite graphic descriptions of persons being resurrected. Three are associated with the prophet Elijah. At 1 Kings 17, he prays for and god raises a young boy. At 2 Kings 4, he raises the son of a woman of Shunem. And, at 2 Kings 13, a dead man, thrown into the dead Elijah's tomb, is resurrected when the man's body touches Elijah's bones.

No resurrection is more pointedly dramatic to the modern mind than Jesus's because of its foundation to the Jesus and Christian stories and is fuller in its telling than those which preceded it. At Matthew 27 we find this account:

> And when Jesus had cried out again in a loud voice, he gave up his spirit. At that moment the curtain of the temple was torn in two from top to bottom. The earth shook, the rocks split, and the tombs broke open. The bodies of many holy people who had died were raised to life. They came out of the tombs after Jesus' resurrection and went into the holy city and appeared to many people.

During the days of and liturgical readings for Easter, how many times have each of us listened to or read those words without grasping their resurrection narrative beyond Jesus's resurrection? This account of many bodies of the saints arose in association with Jesus's resurrection seems worthy of additional commentary in Scripture, but it does not appear beyond Paul's promise in First Corinthians and elsewhere of resurrection awaiting the faithful. John 11 sets out the account of Jesus's raising from the dead Lazarus, brother of the sisters Mary and Martha, said by Martha to Jesus that the tomb holding Lazarus smelled of rotting flesh for he had been dead for four days. As to this, Jesus declared his power to raise Lazarus had come not from himself on Earth but rather from his father in heaven. Mark 5:41 sets forth Jesus's raising the daughter of Jarius also from the dead, not just healing her from an illness.

From its appearance in the teachings, life and death of Jesus, resurrection has been a foundational tenet of the faith. It was a key element in evangelizing to those that had not yet heard Christianity's broader messages. This matters for at least three reasons: Jesus's resurrection means *his* death was sufficient that *our* sins be forgiven, his resurrection means that death is defeated for all persons still living the life accepted for salvation, and his return by resurrection means the life lived on Earth matters to the onward journeys of souls.

Why have Christians not more fully acknowledged the multiplicity of resurrections set out in Scripture? Jesus spoke of them, demonstrated resurrection by performing miracles which included bringing the dead back to life, gave power to his disciples to do them and some did, was resurrected himself, and caused other resurrections to occur in the same Good Friday timeframe. Except at worship on and near Easter and the Nicaean Creed recital, resurrection appears to be an off-limits subject for homilies, sermons and Bible study classes. Are these reluctances consequences of modern theology as nominally professed Christians move from belief in Jesus as the son of God incarnate on Earth to a belief in him as merely a learned ethical teacher of consequence?

Jesus's transfiguration is believed to have prepared him in ways not discernible to us for his approaching death and resurrection and to deepen his disciples' beliefs in whom he said he was, the son of God, the resurrection demonstrating the divine unity of father and son within Jesus, an intersection of another plane of existence with this one. The presence of Moses and Elijah was startling and their discussion with Jesus may have dealt directly with his approaching crucifixion and resurrection. Occurring about six months before those two interconnected events, something else occurred at the transfiguration which may have further infused in him the supernatural powers relevant to his resurrection. Perhaps it was solely a description of that future, but it warrants further examination. It is a focus on the phenomenon of resurrection.

Resurrection is the return to life of the person who has died, whereas reincarnation is a life moving from a body that has physically died to a successive living one. Resurrection appears in Scripture over differing timelines, for example Lazarus after four days, Jesus over three days, and the daughter of Jarius nearly immediately. An indeterminate timeline occurred in the resurrection in Jerusalem of saints at the time of Jesus's crucifixion. The references in Matthew 17, Mark 9, and Luke 9 to Jesus's transfiguration is also of a resurrection event at which two long-past lives appear with Jesus with Peter, James and John at the transfiguration as witnesses to Moses's and Elijah's presences and their speaking with Jesus. How might this event have occurred if not by Moses, among other reasons representing the Law, and Elijah, among other reasons representing prophecy, appearing in their respective afterlives following their long-ago deaths, a millennium and a half in Moses's case and nearly a millennium in Elijah's?

Several books within the Apocrypha, notably the Gospel of Thomas and the Gospel of Mary of Magdala, set out Jesus's description of resurrection to his disciples beyond what we know from the New Testament. They are consistent with the Synoptic Gospels but contribute additional elements. The Gospel of Thomas is regarded by some scholars to be the earliest composed of the gnostic Gospels and with an authorship date as early as the 50s AD. Some have referenced it as the fifth Gospel, but it does not have that placement or stature in the New Testament, but weight may be given to Thomas's account by virtue of his unique, that is doubting, relationship to Jesus. It was to Thomas that the resurrected Jesus made clear he was not a spirit when Thomas doubted his presence, "See my hands and my feet, that it is I myself; touch me and see, for a spirit does not have flesh and bones as you see that I have. And when he had said this, he showed them his hands and his feet."

So, what principally do Thomas and Mary set out as to the potential for resurrection that each attributes to their discussions with Jesus? That the continued existence of the soul does not require any element of a physical human body, thereby answering quite understandable ancient and modern questions concerning bodies' decompositions, cremations, consumptions by beast of forest or field, even skeletons decomposition into surrounding soil, in each instance the soul having departed the physical body following its death. In respect to that timing, there is some scholarship that the Essenes believed it took three days, note that number, for all of the soul's essences to depart a deceased's body. In this description, a person who achieves salvation upon his death, no longer requires further movements of his soul through successive physical human bodies. For a person who does not achieve salvation upon death, does the soul await a final disposition at Judgment Day or does it return in a human body for another opportunity to move toward a perfected state? This question is just that, perhaps a profound one or simply wonderment, and it is posed here to provoke protracted contemplation; it is a question, not an answer.

In the first century AD, momentum from Jesus and his followers' hard work brought forth what would become Christianity for some Jews and some Gentiles. Successor centuries witnessed converts to Christianity on one hand and the survival and growth of the Jewish people on another, both now continuing in those growths. To capture accurately what occurred within Christianity, the analogy of a stream works well. In the image of an initial stream flowing upward instead of tributaries flowing downward into a distributary or a single stream, Christianity's earliest single stream broke into several major distributaries, Roman Catholic, Orthodox, and Protestant, and they continue growing and dividing even now. By the twenty-first century, while Christianity numbered 2.52 billion followers, Catholicism was constituted by 1.3+ billion; Protestantism 900 million, with 300 million to 400 million of their number in historically Protestant faiths, for examples Anglicanism, Baptist, Lutheran, Calvinist, and Methodist and others, but a larger 400 million to 500 million in such faiths as Pentecostal and nondenominational. There are 220 million Eastern Orthodox, with 5.5 million Old Believers, and 62 million in Oriental Orthodox denominations. Modern Messianic Judaism is researched and reported in Christian, not Jewish, numbers at 0.3 million.

In respect to that last description, in the 1800s some Jewish believers in the content of Jesus's teachings began to retake ownership of their Jewish faith by departing from Gentile Christians' interpretations of Scripture and its described events. They returned to Jewish expressions of faith and ritual while remaining outside mainstream Judaism. They challenged aspects of nearly two millennia of Christian interpretations, institutions, rituals and eschatology while still sharing some common foundations with them: faith based on God in heavenly and earthly manifestations, striving to live without sin, repentance following sinful acts, redemption, baptism aligned with repentance, resurrection, and eternal judgment. This particular messianic Judaism is seen as a renewed attempt to fulfill Jesus's original intention to reform Judaism. Others see it in the context of his post-resurrection call of his disciples to the enlarged mission of taking his word to all nations of peoples. Perhaps it is both. There is also in our day Messianic Judaism (Hebrew: יַהֲדוּת מְשִׁיחִית or יהדות משיחית, Yahadút Mešiḥít), a "modernist and syncretic movement of Protestant Christianity that incorporates some elements of Judaism and other Jewish traditions into evangelicalism."

We should now better understand the "well pleased" nature of God the father at Jesus's baptism for God knew and affirmed that Jesus's intended messages after half of a lifetime of preparation were aligned with what God intended them to be. From this affirmation flowed an empowerment of Jesus not only to teach but also to heal as expressions of love for one another. While both would attract, the teaching informing and the healing further convincing, the former persuaded in a ordinary sense and the latter persuaded in a profoundly extraordinary manner. The first was of this world and the second of another. The transfiguration amplified his powers, seemingly connecting another world through him to this one, for even greater proof flowed from his acts after that event.

CHAPTER 8

Jesus and Peter

Not long after the threat at Mount Precipice had passed, Jesus made his way eastward to the Sea of Galilee. His ministry having been launched, he called upon Peter, then known as Simon the son of a Jonah, and Peter's fellow fishermen to join him in that ministry. Jesus began living in Capernaum because that was where Peter and his extended family lived and in doing so Jesus fulfilled Isaiah's prophecy that the messiah would influence two ancient Israeli tribe's locations, Zebulun and Naphtali, more than others. This move would have the consequence of him, his teaching, and his miracles becoming more immediately and far more widely known for another reason, one of geography and commerce. As noted, Via Maris, the major trade route from the Fertile Crescent through Damascus and along its trail north of the Sea of Galilee to the Mediterranean and its ports, brought merchants, caravan drivers, others, and discordant views of matters to the precincts of Capernaum. News of Jesus's preaching, miracles and foretelling of the future went quickly in the directions all were headed. Their accounts carried rightful and wrongful impressions of him and his teaching, but they added risks to him in their expansion.

His nearly twenty-mile walks from Nazareth to the nearest shoreline of Galilee were shorter than walks to Jerusalem. They were also shorter than Joseph and Mary's trek during the late stage of her pregnancy to Bethlehem to be present for the census ordered by Quirinius, the governor of Syria to which Judea had been added by the Romans eager to attain larger numbers of their subjugated populations. This census's date is disputed. Luke referenced it as during the reign of Herod the Great but, while this Herod had died nine years earlier, he was succeeded by his son Herod Archelaus, to which a Herodian family reference may have been what Luke intended and a translator had not understood. Further, Nazareth was not in Judea, giving rise to a possibility Joseph and Mary were not living in Nazareth at the time of the ordering of the census; otherwise, why respond to the census call? There had to be another reason for responding, and where they were living, even if temporarily, might be the answer. Joseph and Mary's travel to Bethlehem was only about six miles longer than their frequent three-day journeys from Nazareth to Jerusalem were; if living elsewhere, perhaps shorter. The poor had few alternatives to walking, the most available being to ride an owned, borrowed, or rented donkey. Persons of financial means might have secured a horse, and the few of great wealth may have secured a four-bearer borne litter or already owned one.

The principal trail between living in Nazareth and working at the shoreline of the Sea of Galilee was well traveled. Persons and their pack animals were accustomed to it. Joseph in his going and returning on this route would have known most all of the Nazarenes he encountered and they him. Living permanently in one place while working temporarily in another could have been for days, weeks or months each time. In the apocryphal Gospel according to James, Jesus shared that he had been told his father was absent from Nazareth for the first three months of Mary's pregnancy. By this account, wherever Joseph was in those months, he was not in Nazareth.

Galilee was busier than ordinarily during certain periods of the year, and planting and harvest seasons intensified activity levels. Agriculture occurred throughout ancient Israel's areas where runoff from winter rain, occasional spring rains, and other sources of accessible water were sufficient for it. The Sea of Galilee dominated fishing. Even if families farmed its arable lands, harvesting from dried grains to succulent grapes, vegetables and fruits, and dates and olives, or they husbanded goats, sheep and cattle, the heads of households and their families would have known how fish were caught by line and by net, for fish were a common food.

The Sea of Galilee's Tiberias, Magdala, Gennesar, Tabgha, and Capernaum were a twenty-plus-mile distance from Nazareth depending to which town a person was walking. It is now a twenty-three-mile motored drive eastward from Nazareth to Magdala. These proximities raise several questions about Joseph. Could his skills, need for additional work, and the nearness of these lakeshore communities, have led him and others in his family to work from time to time in them? More specifically to Jesus's experiences among these communities, could Joseph have become a worker of woods used for the construction of boats, not a boat wright who oversaw construction of the hull, adding later the ribs and installing the planking and all else to deliver a finished boat, but rather someone who did supervised work for and on them? This is a speculation, and not an aimless one, but it is nonetheless a possibility, for it could account for his and his family's knowledge of Galilean places, families, persons, and occupations, and those persons' knowledge of him and them.

What were additional prospects for Joseph and Jesus for building work in these shoreline communities? Older homes would have required restoration and sometimes an additional one or two rooms and the difficult reworking required to connect the new with the old. There was also the need for construction of new housing and outbuildings, such as animal sheds. All were needed for a population moving from other settlements to where netting and processing fish and growing and harvesting crops meant jobs and coin and food stuffs in payment for labor rendered.

A reference in the apocryphal Infancy Gospel of Matthew indicates that Joseph not only did carpentry work in "Capernaum by the sea" but moved his family there, which, if confirmed by future research, would enlarge Joseph's and Jesus's knowledge of Peter's hometown, but we do not need that answer for the account we do know. We should ask ourselves if Joseph's family was living there, why are there other accounts of his family continuing to live in Nazareth? And, if Joseph's family was there, why would Jesus have lived with Peter and his family rather than his own family? An answer to the former may be both accounts are accurate but occurred at different times. An answer to the latter may be that the content of his preaching ostracized him to the extent he and his family accommodated their differences by living apart at least for some time, perhaps early in his ministry.

We can speculate that Joseph temporarily working and living along this shoreline would be a reason why the area, persons, their families, and their livelihoods were known to him and first-hand or second-hand to Jesus. The first four disciples called by Jesus would have more readily followed him if they had already known both whom Jesus was and what he was intending to be the content of his teaching. Peter and Andrew casting nets and James and John mending them had what appears in Scripture to be an instant acceptance of Jesus's call to them, perhaps a divinely inspired reaction, perhaps also because they knew him and trusted him in what he was intending to do, each point reinforcing the other. Peter had an impulsive nature, but giving up his occupation and income would have been at great risk to his family's wellbeing, so his fishing business, for that it was, could have continued under his family's directions and crew's labor. To maintain their standard of living, they probably did, to which they most probably added funding support for his ministry.

Peter, Andrew, and Philip's hometown was Bethsaida, Aramaic for "house of fishing." In observing that meaning, Father Pixner has opined that, if the town had been in England, it would have been named Fishington. This Bethsaida was known during Jesus's time as Bethsaida Julias in order to avoid confusion with another Bethsaida on the north shore of Galilee. Peter's Bethsaida sat on the east bank of the Jordan about one mile upstream from the lake's shoreline. Although Bethsaida was principally a Jewish community, it had also an influential Greek population. Peter moved from Bethsaida to Capernaum because it was his wife's home village, and she had family-tied needs to return to it, although she later accompanied him on some of his mission travels with Jesus.

The pilgrimage authority John Beck noted the historical and faith significance of Capernaum in his observation, "At Capernaum you can walk where Jesus walked and sit next to structures whose stones heard his voice." That's a chill bumps reference to me. Gustaf Dalman concluded that "there is no spot in the whole of Palestine where memories heap themselves up to such an extent as in Capernaum," and he could have substituted "miracles" for memories. That's another one. It was a community of narrow streets with mostly limestone housing interspersed with occasional basalt and marble dwellings. It had a substantial marketplace, an indicator of some affluence. Jesus performed miracles in Capernaum, including curing Peter's mother-in-law who was ill with a severe fever. In the synagogue here, he taught, healed the man with the unclean spirit, and healed on the Sabbath the man with the withered hand. It was here that the centurion came to plead for his sick servant amidst praise from Jewish leaders that he was worthy of Jesus's attention because he had built their synagogue for them. It was here that Jesus discoursed on the meaning of himself as the bread of life. Masterman tells us that this synagogue, at seventy-eight feet in length and fifty feet in width, is the finest among those known from ruins. With the exception of Jesus at his synagogue in Nazareth, Capernaum's is the only one referenced in the Gospels in its relationship to Jesus. He probably entered a synagogue in Magdala, perhaps even teaching in it, its state of preservation exceptional today, its *bet midrash* (study room) quite obvious today in its design, but his preaching there is not referenced in the Bible. Jesus healed others in Capernaum, including those with disorders manifested by recurrent seizures. As he traveled through the region, the infirmed went to him to be healed and crowds flocked to witness the healing of others and hear his spoken message, for widening faith in him and his message of love for one another were among the reasons he healed.

Healing as a restoring to persons to fuller lives can be recalled wrongly as a power limited to Jesus, which it was not, for he instilled it in his disciples and was distraught when he perceived that their inadequate faith in themselves was the cause of their early failures to heal. In time, failure was succeeded by success as demonstrated in Acts 3:1–10:

> One day Peter and John were going up to the temple at the time of prayer—at three in the afternoon. Now a man who was lame from birth was being carried to the temple gate called Beautiful, where he

> was put every day to beg from those going into the temple courts. When he saw Peter and John about to enter, he asked them for money. Peter looked straight at him, as did John. Then Peter said, "Look at us!" So the man gave them his attention, expecting to get something from them.
>
> Then Peter said, "Silver or gold I do not have, but what I do have I give you. In the name of Jesus Christ of Nazareth, walk." Taking him by the right hand, he helped him up, and instantly the man's feet and ankles became strong. He jumped to his feet and began to walk. Then he went with them into the temple courts, walking and jumping, and praising God. When all the people saw him walking and praising God, they recognized him as the same man who used to sit begging at the temple gate called Beautiful, and they were filled with wonder and amazement at what had happened to him.

Jesus's healings affronted Pharisee priests who dismissed them as fakery, even though we can reason that some among their large number, such as Nicodemus, were not of one mind on the Jesus question. Years later, Paul still referred to himself as a Pharisee even after he had set to work to fulfill Jesus's mission. In respect to Jesus's miracles, those who opposed him knew he was doing what they could not, curing those afflicted with maladies and in doing that giving renewed senses of life to those cured. Jews witnessing miracles knew of the intense stress between priests and Jesus, a consequence being it lessened public esteem of the priests and that diminution reduced their influence.

An event which tightened the collaboration of the priests and the governing Romans to rid themselves of Jesus's potential for undesired troublemaking came at a synagogue's service at which a man with a withered, shriveled hand was presented by his friends to Jesus for healing. Jesus challenged the Pharisees among the assembled to declare whether it was lawful or unlawful to do this type of healing on the Sabbath, a challenge with humanitarian intent boldly set against the tenet that healing was allowed on the Sabbath only if it were a matter of life or death and healing a hand was not. Jesus observed the Sabbath, but with the distinction that "The Sabbath was made for man, not man for the Sabbath" (Mark 2:27), that is, its requirements ought not to prevent such acts of love as healing an afflicted person. Knowing the crowd supported this healing, the priests remained silent, and we surmise Jesus that restored the hand in both appearance and function. We also know that Jesus healed others on Sabbaths: he cast out an evil spirit, he made a crippled woman straight, he cured the man with dropsy, and he opened the eyes of a blind man. He reinforced his first words to the priests with "My Father is always at his work to this very day, and I too am working." (John 5:17)

There may be more to this event than the summarizing scriptural account informs us. We know from it that the priests' motivation was not to anger the crowd against them, but we will never know each priest's innermost thoughts for, unexpressed, they could have varied, perhaps appreciably. We do not know with any specificity what their fellow Pharisee Nicodemus may have shared with them as to Jesus's ministry. Whatever they were, how could they not have been awestruck by seeing right before their own eyes this healing, rather than from second- or third-hand accounts of Jesus's miracles, for it demonstrated that the power of God within him was not limited to on which day it was expressed, that healing is worthy on any day it occurs.

Further as to the priests, while silence disguises agreement or disagreement, only the person silent knows which it is, even if they did not disclose subsequently and fully all of their opinions to their superiors in the priesthood. In these respects nonetheless, at the healing of two blind men, the Pharisees present claimed Jesus had not performed that miracle as a demonstration of God's powers but rather of devils. Lastly, were they encompassed within Jesus's asking of the father to forgive them, for they knew not what they were doing? Jesus's later advocate, the English chancellor Sir Thomas More, gave his life by being beheading on this point that silence does not consent or oppose, and earned sainthood in the process. Where is Peter, a central figure in the spread of Jesus's mission, in these moments and other moments?

Peter's birth name was Shim'on (Σίμων in Hebrew), a common name then and now, one meaning "[God] has heard" and modified as a Jewish name of a male child ever so slightly to sound like a similar sounding Greek name, thus Simon. Jesus was to add an additional name to Simon's, a practice not rare in Jewish areas shared with Hellenistic and Roman cultures. He added the Aramaic *Cephas*, meaning rock or stone, some have asserted even a rocky-like tough guy, in its translation into Greek, most Christians assuming a rock or stone large enough to serve metaphorically as a corner foundation stone of a house of wordship, perhaps of an entire faith. Why had Peter been the first to be called by Jesus to his mission? John 1:38–41 informs us that Peter, his brother Andrew, and a Philip, met with Jesus while he was at John the Baptist's encampment near Bethany east of the Jordan, and one or more of them returned to Galilee with Jesus as he recruited his innermost circle.

In time Peter was to become the first in stature among those called, though at times we may have wondered why if the reason had not been set out in Scripture. He leaned too heavily upon his own goals and was far too uncertain in his loyalty from what appears to have been lack of in-depth understanding of Jesus's teachings and weaknesses in his personal courage. He stressed out Jesus more than in mere passing and more than once. In Matthew 16:23 we find what was a low-water mark between them when the transfigured Jesus angrily rebuked Peter with "Get behind me, Satan! You are a stumbling block to me. You do not have in mind the concerns of God, but merely human concerns." We know that was not the worst of it, for in fulfillment of Jesus's prediction Peter denied Jesus three times on the night before Jesus's death, John at 18:15–27 informing us that Peter's fear of arrest or perhaps worse consequences caused him to deny that he even knew Jesus.

While Peter was imperfect in thought, word, and deed, Jesus's choice of him to carry forward the arduous work of his mission may have included an intentional demonstration to each of us, as imperfect as we each are, of Jesus knowing no one of us, then, now or in the future, is perfect. Peter became Simon Peter because Jesus felt Peter's exclamation first from among the assembled disciples, "You are the Messiah," "You are the Christ, "You are the son of the living god," depending on translations, was an exclaimed awareness that Jesus was the divine son of the divine God. Simon Peter became a foundation stone of a Judaic-origined movement consisting of followers of Christ, they later known as Christians and the religious movement known as Christianity, that name given by them and others to the body of religious thought constituted from Jesus's teachings. I imagined in my own youth's Bible study–nurtured contemplation of these events that this transfiguration was like a *chrysalis*, the physical body of Jesus, as the Son of Man to which he would refer to himself, resurrected as a physical confirmation of his nature as the Son of God. Aside from chrysalis as a stage in the transition of a caterpillar to a butterfly, it also means more broadly “a transitional state,” “a stage of being and growth.”

If Jesus did not know fishing with the proficiency of a fisherman before living under Peter’s roof, he would have learned it there. While Peter and his family knew that Jesus was on a mission of far greater significance than catching fish, Jesus’s rhythms of life in Peter’s household would have mirrored the family’s more than theirs his. Joining Peter, members of his family and others in fishing, even if just occasionally or only rarely, would have been a way of showing his gratitude for the shelter in which he slept and the partaking of food and drink at common table, but we have neither written nor any other proof that he fished with them. It is my hunch arising from what we known at the intersection of his personality and their shared culture. As noted previously, *mishpacha*, in Hebrew a member of a family in a non-blood relationship, captures these thoughts. We do know he boated with them for transportation and as a preaching platform.

To explore this possibility further, who among those in or near Peter’s household fished a particular night or an occasional day would have been routine yet occasionally varied by circumstances of the moment, such as a sudden illness. Even though we have no historic account of it, meaning we are left with only logic and the social traditions in Judaism of personal relationships and friendships, might Jesus have fished with them on such an occasion? While Simon and Zebedee were in a joint enterprise of fishing, their two boats and crews working in tandem, especially when seine nets were used, even Peter might not have been with his boat every time it went out, for there were many demands upon him, including the management of the commercial side of his fishing enterprise. Proceeding with an appreciation of social graces, there is at least the possibility that Jesus joined Peter from time-to-time or at least on rare occasions in helping to assure the livelihood which provided for the household in which Jesus was living. He was taught in family and village to help those that toiled, and he was perceptive in thought and strong in body, a combination appropriate for a fisherman's hard labors. A counter argument to this is that occupations were occupations and did not overlap in their highly structured society and its economy.

Jesus, Peter, the disciples, and their families and neighbors spoke primarily Aramaic in their daily lives. Because it is a language that barely survived the centuries which followed the early Christian era, we assume wrongly it almost disappeared because it had been only a local language. Quite to the opposite, Aramaic was then the official and widespread language of the vast Achaemenid Empire, the language of Darius the Great, his powerful son Xerxes and hundreds of thousands more. Its name derives from the ancient Middle Eastern people known as Aramaeans. It was closely related to Hebrew and had begun supplanting it among Jews as early as the sixth century BC. It was close to the Syriac and Phoenician languages too, and it was a common language in much of what were to become the Holy Lands for the Achaemenid Empire had encompassed that region for centuries. It survives in our twenty-first century only in some Syrian villages, but its East Aramaic derivation is still spoken by small groups of Jacobite and Nestorian Christians in the Middle East. In Jesus's time it was indeed a widely spoken language and in many places the language of the street.

We return to the Aramaic-speaking Jesus and Peter in Capernaum. Peter was in the business of selling fish for coin, barter or both and doing so surrounded by complexities which cannot be overlooked, their details required for understanding them. As noted earlier, the Hebrew term, *g'lil ha-goyim* is evidence that the area was inhabited in part by Gentiles at least at the time the Book of Hebrews was composed and that term used, and long after it. Greeks who followed Alexander the Great's 332 BC subdued conquest of Judea left deep cultural imprints on it. Hellenism, the Greek way of life, influenced the Pharisees on key points of view before and during Jesus's lifetime.

While Hellenism had found common religious ground in the East, made easier by their and Eastern polytheisms, it was only partially successful among monotheistic Jews, a belief in the possibility of afterlife finding some acceptance among the Pharisees. As prior colonizers of this region, Greeks were seen by the Roman colonizers as enculturated locals, both Greeks and Romans ingratiating themselves at the expense of the indigenous population. The Romans tolerated the jurisdictional divisions between Jews and Samaritans but, because the Jews' respect of the Sabbath meant that they would police on only the remaining 86 percent of each week, the Romans chose their policing troops primarily from Samarians. Where does this discussion of languages take us?

In that Peter and his family were catchers of and Peter was a seller of most of the fish caught, he made a first century living at it. He spoke Aramaic in his daily life and Hebrew in his temple life, but the selling of fish required some level of language skills beyond those. Raised in Bethsaida, a community with a Greek population, he almost certainly understood and spoke some Greek and given the pervasive Roman occupation some if not much Latin, this multiplicity of four languages a necessity for him as for others. As a revealing example of the mixed cultures and languages of the region, Jesus used the Greek, neither Aramaic, Hebrew, nor Latin, word for actor, *hypocrite*, twenty-four times in the Gospels in referring to persons with insincere religiosity.

Growing into adulthood in a Roman-occupied land, Jesus would have understood some Latin too, though he asked for translation of the Latin inscription on a Roman coin shown to him by agitated Pharisee priests as they tried to entrap him in sedition, but the circumstances of that moment may have been a pretense by him of not knowing any Latin in order to avoid effectively the direct answer they sought and thought they were going to get. The long march of world history informs us that the conquered learn to speak the conqueror's language more necessarily than conquerors learn the language of the conquered. Facility in multiple languages can be a key to assimilation, a social byproduct sometimes effectively reducing cultural and other tensions. In Galilee, being able to understand, such as a Roman soldier shouting "Prohibere!" meaning "Stop!" as well as thinking and speaking in, the languages surrounding your life was a useful and valued requirement of daily living.

In these respects where was the center of the Sea of Galilee's western shore value-added processing of fish netted by Peter, Zebedee, and others for sale and transport to domestic and foreign markets? It was in Magdala, where the trail, including the Wadi el-Hamam section which Jesus walked from Nazareth, met the Sea of Galilee. It was a long-established community, for the priestly order of Ezekiel is believed to have had its seat in Magdala from the sixth century BC, and it was in Jesus's time a bustling commercial center.

The relationship between Jesus and Mary of Magdala, this community, began in the uncustomary manner of his miraculous healing of her. Unlike the healed about which we know nothing in Scripture as to what occurred later in their lives, we know much about hers. She is mentioned by name twelve times in the Gospels, which is more than most of the disciples and more than any other woman outside Jesus's family. She appears to have developed a close relationship with Jesus's mother. She is often mentioned in gnostic writings, a thread through them being Jesus's confiding in her beyond what he shared in discussions with his male disciples, probably because he knew she understood him and his teachings at greater depth than did they, perhaps because her questions reflected that depth.

Visiting Magdala warrants, in our years it demands, historically accurate commentary on Mary Magdalene. Mark and Luke describe Jesus healing her from a neurologically manifested disorder, perhaps epilepsy, maybe severe migraine bouts. Scripture also refers to possession by seven demons though commentaries suggest that number may have its origin more in Jewish culture than in her malady. Her response was sustained appreciation as she became one of a small number of women, including Peter's wife, who accompanied Jesus and his disciples and supported them from their own resources, perhaps an indication Mary was a widow with some financial means. This would explain also why she was free from men in her family any longer controlling her life.

While there has been speculation that she learned of Jesus and his mission through Magdala's fish processing work places, her self-sufficiency may have originated otherwise in textile-weaving, pigeon raising or other of Magdala's many enterprises. As to her uniqueness in the life of Jesus, unlike any other person healed by him, she was with his mother and only one disciple, believed to be John the Beloved, at his crucifixion. Further, she was the first woman to see inside the empty tomb in which Jesus had been laid. At that tomb and amidst her confusion as to where the body might have been stolen and taken, Jesus gained her attention by calling her by name, to which she responded, and then by speaking directly to her, after which she returned to the disciples to proclaim "I have seen the Lord." That made her the first to inform them of the astonishing news of his resurrection. It would be 1969 before the Roman Catholic Church recognized publicly that she was not the sinful woman who had come to Jesus as a penitent.

Scorned for many centuries as a prostitute or at least a promiscuous woman, we now know that a mistaken understanding caused this most grievous error, one which endured for centuries and even to this day. Regrettable but not surprisingly, it is a common malady in any culture that mistruth often outlives or at least overpowers truth. Nonetheless, it would have been instructive to those thinking of following the Word of Jesus if she had been a prostitute and Jesus had treated her with publicly visible forgiveness and respect. The often expressed point that he came to save sinners, not saints not needing his intervention, comes to my mind.

Magdala's identification with fish was so extensive that it was known in Hebrew as *Migdal Nunaya*, Fisherman's Tower, for it was the site of a lighthouse to aid watermen in their nighttime navigation on the lake, including especially their return to the city's docks before daybreak. Excavations begun here in the 1970s were interrupted but begun again in 2006 with the cooperation of the Israeli Antiquities Authority. The ruins of the village of Mary's day had been covered with only several feet of debris and soil, disguising its precise location, size and urban complexity but easing that later excavation. Magdala's prosperity in the biblical era was built on the industry of many of its subjects in their drying, salting and otherwise preserving fish to assure that they did not spoil in their either short overland to domestic or lengthy overland and sea journeys to overseas markets in often stifling ambient temperatures. Near where fishing boats anchored, the stone-slabbed flooring of the fish marketplace ran along the shoreline where lead weights from nets and bronze fish hooks have been unearthed.

Andrea Garza-Díaz described the Magdala of Mary's time as a wealthy Jewish town, for no other one in that area had elaborate ritual baths (*miqva'ot*), "a synagogue with mosaic floors, or a hydraulic system with water flowing through its channels." While it was later attacked and partially destroyed by the Romans, it survived the occupation. After all, Romans as well as locals wanted Galilean fish on their plates. The Greeks had known Magdala as Trachea, meaning "fish curing," and the Greeks in some periods even referred to the inland sea itself by that name.

Magdala's place in history is not only assured by Scripture but also by the contemporary writings of Flavius Josephus, Cicero, Pliny the Elder, Strabo, and Suetonius to cite the most notable. Josephus wrote it was a city of 40,000 inhabitants, a highly questionable number to archaeologists digging and this pilgrim, me, looking over where the fish market and processing center, boatbuilding yards and sheds, and various other industries were located. It was the originating site of a fish condiment so popular among gourmands in Rome as to be singled out by Strabo, an educated citizen of the Roman Empire of Greek descent and the compiler of the encyclopedic *Geographica* (εωγραφικά). Magdala was a major contributor of taxes to revenue-hungry governments. It was a Greek monk, Epiphanius, who reported in the seventh century that a church, some have written a basilica, had been built as early as 325 AD by Helena, Emperor Constantine's mother, on the locals-believed site of Mary Magdalene's house. Magdala then is Migdal now on printed maps and in GPS navigational aids.

The Saint John Paul II–inspired Magdala Center now complements the expanded tradition-steeped papal center of Notre Dame of Jerusalem and its accommodations for the conveniences of pilgrims. I have stayed there with fellow pilgrims, and I recommend it for those and shared conversation purposes. During his May 2009 pilgrimage to the Holy Lands, Benedict XVI blessed this Magdala Center's cornerstone, the construction of which had to be permitted by Israeli authorities in conjoined church and state recognitions. This center is intended to bolster the Vatican's "bridges of dialogue between the faithful of the different religions in the Holy Land," a site of encounter and prayer for clergy and pilgrims alike. Father Joan Solano, the director of this Notre Dame, believed from the intersection of archeological, geographical and scriptural evidences that Jesus's *Talitha cumi*—"Little girl, rise!" raising of the synagogue leader Jarius's daughter from the dead took place in Magdala, not in Capernaum as asserted by other scholars, in that Magdala is between Tabgha where Jesus was and Nazareth and there are no other synagogues in that route and Capernaum was six miles in a different direction.

Notre Dame de Jerusalem is a short walk from the Damascus Gate entry to the old walled city and then to the Via Dolorosa, the winding Sorrowful Way from Jesus's imprisonment at Antonia Fortress to the site of his crucifixion at Golgotha, that latter distance of about 2,000 feet.

Amidst its shadowed precincts, Peter hid that night for fear of arrest, but that act of self-preservation was within weeks addressed by Jesus's reinforcement of him by intently directed words of encouragement. The only somewhat longer Greek Orthodox pilgrimage route to Golgotha begins each Good Friday on top of the Mount of Olives, pauses in Gethsemane on its eastern slope, crosses the deepest point of the Kidron valley, climbs its western hillside at the top of which is the wall and eastern side of Temple Mount, and enters the Old City through the fabled Lion's Gate. It then follows the Via Dolorosa to the Church of the Holy Sepulcher now encompassing the sites of Jesus's crucifixion. Although neither Greek by heritage nor Greek Orthodox by faith, though it is tempting, I have walked with Greek and American friends in their procession along what now constitutes the Via Dolorosa and for a stretch carrying, as did others in turn, a replicated cross lighter than the much heavier one borne and haltingly dragged by a much stronger Jesus.

A friend for decades, fellow pilgrim and demonstrated scholar in the life of Jesus believes Jesus did not enter Jerusalem on Palm Sunday through the Lion's Gate. Rather, he believes the Lamb of God, especially knowing he was headed to his orchestrated murder, would have entered through the Sheep's Gate which is around the 90± degree turn in the ancient wall which gate was used for entrance of lambs and sheep being ushered to the Temple for ritual sacrifice. I believe the pathway from this gate and the Lion's Gate intersect in a manner which preserves the traditional notions of palms and branches along the Via Dolorosa. This gate's sheep for sacrifice purpose is referenced in Nehemiah 3:1 of which Jesus would have had full knowledge.

Peter's roles in the spreading of Jesus's good news became many and, when he and others were called by Jesus to be fishers of followers in that good news, his knowledge as fisherman was quite relevant, and the disciples took it with them into their new tasks. But, there is a deeper, more meaningful account which arises here for a necessary understanding by Christians.

Following his crucifixion and resurrection, Jesus's fishers of fish whom he intended to become fishers of men had returned to their boats in Galilee. We know this because Jesus found them there, an indication of either their uncertainty as to what to do next in order to extend his name, mission and teachings when he was no longer physically present to lead them or how to prioritize elements of that doing. We cannot overlook the significance of what was a deeper reason. John 12 sets out a fundamental factor in that uncertainty: "But though he had performed so many signs before them, yet they were not believing in him." Did they not believe sufficiently to undertake promptly and persuasively the mission he had defined for them? Aware of this possibility, Jesus took two actions, one right there and a second half a dozen years later, to reinforce then and doubly reinforce later his disciples and especially their Peter as the leader previously chosen by him for that task.

First, he caused a new miracle to occur, one tied directly to their knowledge as fishermen. It was the third time he appeared to them after his resurrection. He appeared at the near shore to seven disciples, including Peter, who had been fishing through the night and catching nothing. This was at Tabgha, a small stretch of Galilean shoreline well known to him and them, for it was here that he had first called them to join him. This particular early morning would anchor through the ages the faith of those that follow his teachings.

Jesus asked the seven if they had any fish, and they answered they did not. He then directed them to cast their net on the right side of the boat for they would find fish there. Disappointed at the lack of a night's catch and exhausted from their trying, they nonetheless did what he directed rather than saying no to someone not yet recognized by them. Albeit not set out in Scripture and not to diminish this as the miracle it was, Galilean fishermen were accustomed to having their movements on the water suggested by someone on shore whose line of sight to water surface disrupted by fish was different from those on the boat. They did as he asked and were not able to draw the net in easily for the multitude of fishes within it. A disciple, most widely believed to have been John, recognized Jesus and said to Peter whom it was. Peter put on his fisher's coat for he had been naked, a lack of attire which would not have been uncommon given the possibly high temperature, the wet nature of water and slippery nature of fish oils, and he began coming ashore. Jumping into the water to assist the progress of a net toward a shore was a common practice. Peter was followed by the disciples bringing the boat, net, and a 153 fish by Scripture's precise account to shore, an accomplished reality, a lesson in following Jesus's directives, and a well-intended allegory of the rewards of proselytizing in Jesus's name.

Once on shore they noticed that Jesus was cooking fish, almost certainly tilapia because of its prevalence in the lake, at a charcoal fire on an outcropping of limestone rock, and that he had bread with him. He shared that fish and bread with them as a breakfast, and a discussion followed whose momentum became historic. Jesus's declaration of the primacy of Peter was reinforced here as it needed to be in the wake of Peter's behavior on the night before Jesus's crucifixion, his personal fear obvious to other disciples. Jesus's reinforced Peter's primacy by this one-on-one discussion observed by those disciples.

Almost certainly looking intently into his eyes, as is the case in such instances, Jesus posed three-times to Peter: "Do you love me more than you love others?" It was a way of Jesus asking him but in his different words, *Peter, can I count on you?* Peter's responses were each time yes but, by the third time it was asked, Peter may have been exasperated, though he should not have been given his own recent disappointing behavior. Peter responded to Jesus's admonitions to "Feed my lambs," "Feed my sheep," and again "Feed my sheep" by acknowledging he understood the commitment Jesus required of him. The circle of Jesus's intensions as to these disciples which began at this shoreline was thus closed, as in bonded forever, in the same place. On August 27, 2022, Pope Francis captured this discussion in his homily addressed to the College of Cardinals at the consistory at which twenty were added to their number:

> The Lord wants to bestow on us his own apostolic courage, his zeal for the salvation of every human being, without exception. He wants to share with us his magnanimity, his boundless courage and unconditional love, for his heart is afire with the mercy of the Father.

Jesus and Peter's understanding here linked the past with their present and added momentum to the mission ahead, and it was in the nature of a simile which we should not overlook. It's how an aged person often acts differently from how he did when he was younger. When younger, an older person advised the younger what to do; when older, the roles flip, and the younger advises the older. Having to do with their relationship, not with their ages, Jesus was advising Peter his leadership was essential to the informing of local faith communities of the message which in time would become a universal community but also that this leadership would be at great risk to him. Peter emerged from his thrice denial of knowing Jesus and being with his entourage and this post-resurrection discussion "as a man humbled and assured, his confidence placed fully in Christ, not himself." Though Peter probably did not grasp it at this moment, Jesus was foretelling Peter that what was to be his later death in Rome should not be feared because a better place awaited him. His death too was by crucifixion, but upside down at Peter's own request in order that it would not be in the same manner as Jesus's in Jerusalem. Yet, before that occurred, Peter's leadership was demonstrated, including by the words which brought many to Jesus's teachings and by miracles performed in Jerusalem with widespread visibility, as are set out in Acts following the four Gospels.

From Peter and Paul's understandings of Jesus's way and their and others' work with the lives of those with a shared view of humanity, Christianity succeeded by way of Jesus's mission, in some measure because of the challenges to it from its first appearances. While those challenges strengthened it, the mission remains fulfilled in part and unfulfilled in part. The sixteenth-century Roman Catholic Papal Basilica of St. Peter at the Vatican is a monument to the faith and work of this Galilean fisherman Peter, as the nineteenth century San Paolo dentro le Mura, St. Paul's Within the Walls, in Rome is a monument to Paul's faith and work in that process. As biblical scholars highlight, roughly half of the New Testament consists of the missionary work which broadened the audience and acceptance of what Jesus had left with them. These recognitions are an appropriate point to discuss more fully the outgrowth of Christianity from the Judaism of the first Christian century.

The Franciscan Order's Church of the Primacy of Saint Peter is now at this Tabgha site on the northwest shore of the sea, the stone outcropping on which Jesus cooked their breakfast now housed within it. It encompasses the ruins of a fourth-century church known into the ninth century as the Place of the Coals, the stone itself venerated as *Mensa Christi*, the Table of Christ, to some and *Mensa Domini*, the Table of God, to others. There are two other such "tables" relevant to Jesus in this area, one at the nearby Church of the Multiplication of the Loaves and Fishes, usually shortened in daily parlance to the Church of the Multiplication, and a third at Mensa Christi Church in Nazareth. This original Church of the Primacy of Saint Peter was destroyed in 1263 AD, having survived longer than any other original Christian church in the region, but it was later rebuilt by those aware of its importance, and it is there now.

While Scripture emphasizes that they followed him, for they did, others who remained at their boats continued the tasks of fishing and generating income from it, some of which almost certainly supported Jesus's mission. It was too valuable an occupation and asset for their families to abandon. This is important for a reason seldom discussed. Jesus and his disciples and others serving along with them could not have traveled throughout the region for three years by living solely off the land or the gratitude of those responding to his message. This retinue was not small in number even if not all persons associated with the early ministry were present at all times. Peter's and Zebedee's boats' crews continued fishing would have provided some of the funds necessary to support Jesus's growing ministry.

Second and about six years later, Jesus singled out Saul of Tarsus, Paul to us, as he was traveling on the road to Damascus, for the critically important role of further strengthening Peter and his disciples in ways set out in Acts. Saul had been ruthless in his persecution of Christians, that contrasting vividly with his future. Jesus declared as to him: "This man is my chosen instrument to proclaim my name to the Gentiles and their kings and to the people of Israel." Jesus bringing Paul into the ministry must have been necessary for why else would it have occurred?

CHAPTER 9

The Foundation of Christianity

The prominence in the world community of Jesus's message attests to it having overcome powerful oppositions, including those which continue in both the secular and spiritual spheres of the modern age. While his ministry was initially framed by its Jewish contexts and roots, it grew in responses to his message, the work of his disciples and then other Jewish followers, they not aware what was happening was the emergence of what became known as Christianity. His message spread by word of mouth and later writings, each and altogether encouraging believers to take risks in the certainty of the truth of his promises.

Two millennia later, Christians' knowledge of Judaism is unfortunately incomplete, and Jews' knowledge of Christianity is similarly so. Both situations are understandable for each's followers live predominantly within their own faith. Christians draw encouragement from the intersection of Jesus's "Do not think that I have come to abolish the Law or the Prophets; I have not come to abolish them but to fulfill them," and his later reference to

Isaiah 57 that his house would be called a house of prayer for all the nations.

Jesus was born into, learned from, reflected, and taught in the period of Second Temple Judaism. He knew full well the differences between the dominant Sadducees and Pharisees, but he also knew the Essenes in their rejection of the teachings and life styles of both Sadducees and Pharisees and knew further of the self-marginalized Zealots. Influences on him were near (Nazareth and Sea of Galilee communities), far (Jerusalem), and many. It is logical to conclude that Jesus's years between twelve and thirty, almost wholly unknown to us, encompassed the sorting out of these influences and the drawing of conclusions from them as they related to his approaching public expressions of them. In that context, we find Jesus's revealing conclusions in Matthew 25 and elsewhere of his intention to do for others what we would have them do for him, intending this and other guidance to be accepted and assimilated by those that welcomed his words.

In the Beatitudes in what we know as his Sermon on the Mount, Jesus set out (Matthew 5–7) nine groupings of persons whom the God of Deuteronomy 18:18 and he knew to be worthy of being blessed. Describing situations in which the blessing may be most personally experienced, they exhort those hearing them to live in ways which led to them and to take heed that failure to do so will have consequences. Paul captured this in his letter to the Corinthians as God having before and here chosen the weak to make the strong aware of that circumstance.

They were the poor in spirit who needed to be lifted from dismay to hopefulness. Those that mourned needed to be comforted by knowing another life had awaited deceased loved ones. The meek who may have sensed their temporal world was passing but an eternal one could be gained. They that hungered and thirsted that they would know that neither they nor others lived by food and drink alone for there was a centralizing spiritual dimension to their lives. The merciful because they had compassion and demonstrated it to others by their supportive actions in respect to them. The pure in heart because they were free from wrongful desires. The peacemakers because they engendered respect within and among families, communities and peoples, that respect a doorway to a deeper depth of love. They that had been persecuted for righteousness' sake because their faith was so deep it was not abandoned for neither convenience nor gain, not even for continued life in this world. We read ourselves or hear others read aloud these Beatitudes, but seldom do we read or hear them explained as they are set out here in answering at least some of the whys as to them.

Benedict XVI has written that "they orient us toward our final end and the purposes of our existence, yet they are not just about thinking of the future, but about living now in the firm hope of the future." Jesus had phrased it more emphatically: "Rejoice and be glad, because great is your reward in heaven" (Matthew 5:12) if you follow them. This view has at times been misconstrued as the framework for a utopian political agenda, but that conclusion ignores Jesus's self-descriptions that he had not come to be a political leader in the mold of David.

There is something else important to this deeper understanding, and that is what they have in common with Jesus to such an extent he made them a central intention of himself and his ministry. It is his personal identification with each in all the categories of the persons described, for they reflect his growing up, young adulthood and learning from within the cultural strata where the poor in spirit, the meek, and the hungry and thirsty were ever present in his own community and in the places to which he traveled and taught. There were the mourners, the merciful, the pure in heart and the peacemakers were found and further sought in all strata of life.

There is a personality characteristic in the Beatitudes worthy of particular focus. It may well have been key to his thinking. It is the feeling of *aloneness* which each or several realities can provoke, a deeply held, self-felt isolation from others from the momentary sensation to the ever present. Jesus intended to free them from that aloneness when he promised them he was with them "until the end of time," a one-with-one comfort that they would never, ever again need to feel alone as in uncared for, friendless, lonesome, lonely, detached, isolated, removed, separated. He not once promised a person that he would not die an earthly death, but he did assuredly promise each that he would be with them every step of their way, always and under every circumstance. That awareness was intended to be a comfort to each, even and especially in the worst of their circumstances. By guiding us on how to live, he was guiding us on how to approach death, a certainty in every instance, but one sought to be comforted by the knowledge of death as a transition to another realm. This message, when heard, was comfortingly transcendent in that it rose above the travails of daily life, again and again and again. How did he move this message into the thoughts of those hearing it? How is it relevant now?

Jesus taught through the uses of parables, elaborating on points made by him, and metaphors sometimes more easily understood by the listeners in that they are figures of speech in which a word or combination of them denote an idea used in place of another to suggest a likeness between them. In his telling of the judgment of persons, known as the parable of the sheep, he described the separation of sheep and goats as a metaphor for the dividing of the blessed and the damned, and those listening knew he was not referring to sheep and to goats. Of course they knew that the blood of a lamb was shed to save the Hebrews at the first Passover on the eve of their exodus from Egypt, its annual recognition becoming the first divine ordinance recorded in Exodus. In Christianity, Jesus is the paschal, meaning Passover, lamb sacrificed by crucifixion to atone for the sins of the world. Jesus also used examples of commendable personal conduct in daily life as they too are set forth in Matthew 25: feeding the hungry, giving drink to the thirsty, sheltering the stranger, clothing those in that need, and visiting prisoners and perhaps, by inference, others confined to the circumstance of loneliness, such as the self-isolated depressed and the aged and largely abandoned ill. These acts are to be done by persons for others as if they were done by those others for the first party, but Jesus made clear that good works alone would not assure salvation, for obedience of the commandments, repentance for transgression, and forgiveness were also required for the good life lived in his name and to be recognized at death.

This is a central point often failed to be expressed by church leaders in the secular world in which they and we live. Worshipping congregations must recall Jesus's call to save souls as they undertake social service work. Rejoice in both.

Jesus's teachings have critical elements, each strong in itself, but strongest together. One is his response to Peter's question: "Lord, if my brother keeps on sinning against me, how many times do I have to forgive him? Seven times?" to which Jesus responded as found in Matthew 18: "No, not seven times, but seventy times seven," which point was far more than a suggestion. As found in Matthew 6, "if you forgive other people when they sin against you, your heavenly Father will also forgive you. But if you do not forgive others their sins, your Father will not forgive your sins." Jesus was instructing us to learn from the offense and directing us to forgive the offender, in our parlance move on, for it is future conduct that will be changed from that learning in that you cannot change what is past, only perceptions of it. His solution removes it beyond discretionary on the aggrieved party's part, for he made it clear that forgiving others as an expression of love is a mandatory action to better prepare the soul for judgment. Some may regard that consequence of failure to forgive as profoundly harsh, but Jesus saw forgiving as the necessary, the essential act of love, thus it is a binding agent. We find it at John 15: "This is my commandment: Love each other," and we should not overlook the gravity of the word commandment. These requirements are powerful because they are centrally important and extraordinarily difficult to achieve, but they also open the door to the greatest of rewards when accomplished habitually.

They may sound quite right to our ears, especially if we think of the twined requirements to forgive and to love, but do we? Who among us does, truly act this way and, if we do, beyond rarely or occasionally? Do we live in this manner in the many instances in our lives in which they are required? I suspect Jesus is disappointed in a Christian who speaks to the importance of forgiveness but in fact does not unconditionally forgive, later still holding a grudge against a person for something suspected or known to have occurred in family or neighborhood, at work, even at church. People may forgive but not forget, without which there is no true forgiving. Deep in their heart, though seldom on their tongue, they still want to get even with the person they feel aggrieved by. Unfortunately, it's a wellspring of thoughts of retribution instead of the source of true forgiveness. While I seek forgiveness within my family, social groupings and other personal and professional acquaintances for my transgressions against them, I must first demand of myself my forgiveness of them and, if and when I fail, I must be contrite and seek forgiveness from Jesus for the failure on that first part is a transgression against him and pray that his atonement for my sins and his unlimited grace will avail me of salvation. In all of this, we understand that the unilateral forgiveness of another is a key to unlocking the love for one another that is the capstone of Jesus's ministry. You control your own life best by forgiving and moving on, not by remaining captive in thought to another's slap, insult or whatever, for in that failure the other person controls you.

In this context of forgiveness as an alternative to retribution Christians can misunderstand Judaism's "Eye for eye, tooth for tooth, hand for hand, foot for foot" (Exodus 21:24) as startlingly harsh, yet they are less harsh than what unlimited revenge might cause to happen in the absence of these anatomical equivalents of graphic imagery then and now. If you plucked out the eye of someone, by this code they could do no more than pluck out one of yours; that is, they could not pluck out both or otherwise maim or kill. There is logic in the belief they are also deterrents but, while not all agree rational deterrents overcome irrational emotion, deterrent is a foundational basis of much of the rule of law. If you are intent on knocking out someone's tooth, you need to recall the aggrieved person's allowed retribution is to knock out your tooth. Thus, all were limitations on personal conduct, their intention being to prohibit reactive conduct worse than originating conduct. In time in Judaism, restitution in alternative values, including monetary values and other acts of contrition, took the place of anatomical equivalents. That notwithstanding and in contrast to all of these forms of restitution, Jesus directed his followers to do neither:

> You have heard that it was said, "Eye for eye, and tooth for tooth." But I tell you, do not resist an evil person. If anyone slaps you on the right cheek, turn to them the other cheek also. And if anyone wants to sue you and take your shirt, hand over your coat as well. If anyone forces you to go one mile, go with them two miles. Give to the one who asks you, and do not turn away from the one who wants to borrow from you.

This seems nearly impossible to do, but Jesus was placing the love of God for all persons above a person's need for vengeance, and this concept separated him fundamentally from centuries of Judaic law and tied culture based on equivalency. The good counsel of Jesus here goes beyond being slapped on the face, albeit a graphic example, for in the contexts of all his counsel, it must mean any offense, whether that is his slap in the face or any other physical act, or a verbal assault such as an insult. We know that if the Law of Moses were followed, the commandments obeyed, offensive acts giving rise to retribution in any form would be reduced. So as to not misconstrue, as many Christians and others often do, what Jesus was illustrating in his words "turn to him the other also," was both an admonishment not to use physical force in retribution but rather use the potential for genuine resolution of a grievance found in the power of words. In short, Jesus was instructing us to move on, turning the other check in doing that, and most often a tension-reducing act at that. Personally, I have found Jesus's *Father, forgive them, for they know not what they do* admonition to be an immediately available and effective thought in my struggles to turn the proverbial other cheek. I have succeeded a few times and failed far more often, but I continue to try. Temper has to have its place, as demonstrated by Jesus himself.

These teachings were sufficiently outside the dominant narrative to have separated the first followers of Jesus from other Jews. Early followers of Jesus were disaffected from the two mainstreams of Judaism, albeit there were more than two streams, and Jesus's message began attracting the attention of Gentiles as well. Judaism was displaced as the mandated religion of Judea and of Galilee by the Roman destruction of the Second Temple in 70 AD, the supplanting of their faith by Rome's pagan beliefs and rituals, and by the resulting dispersal in large part but not altogether of Jews from these lands. These events reduced tensions between Romans and Jews for the principal reason that they reduced the Jews' numbers and thereby their capacities to influence. During the earlier rule of the Emperor Claudius,s Jews had been expelled from Rome, which undertook other harsh measures too, but Judaism survived against outrageously difficult circumstances, grew in numbers and renown, and in my case deep respect. Christianity too was ruthlessly suppressed by Rome before it gained an official status fostered by conversion of the Eastern emperor's mother from which it grew.

CHAPTER 10

Galilean Boats Were Important to Jesus

Jesus's knowledge of what his disciples did when they fished in the Sea of Galilee could not have been insignificant. Disciples knew their boats and nets and contrived and deployed strategies and tactics to secure catches, the more bountiful in number the better for them. He and they knew fishing was a vibrant commerce in the region. Fishing was an ancient skill, almost certainly as old as hunting what lived on land and in air, and in time much of fishing was from boats. Fishing from boats would have been a quite logical reason to be on but not in water for those boats got you closer to where the fish were. The largest of the nets were deployed from and brought in mostly over boats' sterns, intended to be laden with fish of species and sufficient size not to be returned to the water. That act reflects an early awareness of fishery conservation, for only some species of fish and from them only those large enough to be eaten by the catchers and their families and/or sold at the shore's intake facilities were kept on board.

A quandary then and now arises from which netted fish to keep and take to market, a decision running from ancient to modern times, one arising out of the conundrum that the largest, most mature fish have the greatest commercial value yet are the ones most needed to remain in the water to breed additional fish for future harvests. There was another important distinction for Jews: tilapia and other pelagic, meaning living mostly near the water's surface, fish were kosher while catfish and other bottom feeders were proscribed from being eaten by observant Jews, though they could be sold to Romans, Greeks, and other Gentiles.

Surrounded by modern life as we are, many persons, probably most, wrongly believe ancients were not too smart. They are correct in acknowledging the slow accumulation of knowledge, but the ancients enlarged their understandings through deductive and inductive reasonings arising from their own and others' experiences, even if they did not dwell on that dichotomy. Their hands-on experiences at the many tasks of life enlarged their knowledge during each's lifetime, and each generation's new lessons learned expanded the baseline of knowledge for follow-on generations. The overarching restraint was the reality that progressions in fields of learning and their interactions with other fields were gradual. Yet, what they knew about their earthly, oceanic and celestial worlds is well worth recognition in the modern era.

Nearly 50,000 years ago, Neanderthals in Europe wove natural fibers with strengthening patterns so intricate in their making of rope, sometimes used for netting, they survived to this day and astonish modern designers. Nearly 5,000 years ago, the 6-million-ton Great Pyramid of Giza was built with 2.3 million blocks of stone, some weighing eighty tons each, with an engineering accuracy of an astounding one-fourth of an inch at its square base, and it was not a one-off project, for additional pyramids arise in landscapes along the Nile running from Egypt southward into Sudan. The ancients did not need our global positioning satellites (GPS) systems because they traveled on land and navigated by the sun and the stars for great distances. Ancients elsewhere designed the pre-Columbian Mayan calendar with 18,980 unique date correlations to identify each day in a fifty-two-plus-year cycle. Were they ignorant? Obviously not. So, too, the architectural Seven Wonders of the Ancient World were neither conceived, planned, designed nor built by numbskulls.

During the Mesopotamian and Egyptian civilizations, paralleling one another from the thirty-first century BC until the mid-Roman period of Jesus's life, even though they were only about a thousand miles apart geographically, fishing too had become increasingly sophisticated. The Euphrates and the Nile rivers, inhabited by protein-laden finned creatures, challenged this progress to be made to offset declines in other food resources.

Fish were a convenient natural resource, a source of protein, whose capture was far less risky to life and limb than bringing down a beast of forest, field or desert and far less costly and troublesome than raising domesticated animals. While perhaps never thought this way by fishermen plying their trade, fishing may have been regarded as less hard work than plowing and planting fields and harvesting and processing the products which came from them. The reward for effort was more immediate in fishing than in agriculture or animal husbandry. Fish were almost certainly first caught by hand or more probably, if you have tried it yourself you will know this to be true, by many hands. Woven baskets may have been the next technique but, inasmuch as water and fish are pushed away by tightly woven baskets moving rapidly in water toward them, baskets woven with open areas to let water flow through and fish into them may have been the genesis of the concept of woven and tied netting. To that end, the combination of boats and nets considerably decreased degrees of difficulty in catching large numbers of fish.

Features of the fishing boats at the Sea of Galilee were a speculation until as recently as the 1980s, and there had been hundreds of them. Mosaic depictions of that period were little more than crude renderings, even though one mosaic discovered at Artiburus, a Roman–Berber town of Jesus's time in what is now Tunisia westward on the Mediterranean, depicted twelve different designs of boats, each design with a distinctive name reference. Representations on canvas by artists centuries later were based on design elements they knew from their own times. Basic differences were known of course, for example distinctions between working boats and pleasure crafts. Fundamental elements were based upon the intended principal use, ranging from the transportation of heavy and bulky cargos or many persons and whatever accompanied them, through the commerce of fishing, to recreational sailing and rowing crafts. Owners lived with the stark reality that any or all of their boats could be requisitioned on a moment's notice by civil or military authorities, and the owner might or might not have been successful in getting them returned or receiving fair or any compensation when not.

Galilean fishing boats could be rowed, sailed, or both. The boats used by Peter and his fishermen had deep, rounded sterns and fine bows with an upward bowsprit but it was neither as tall nor as representationally carved as a Viking longboat's. Their centered single masts were erected at a nearly ninety-degree angle to the water surface. The sail of each, when unfurled and held by multiple brail lines worked through that age's version of cleats attached to the caprail at its aft mid-section, gave relief to rowers. Assuming compatible weather, sailing was used for achieving greater distances in contrast to rowing for close-in work, such as deploying and retrieving nets, as well as when there was no wind and for departing from and returning to dock or shore in darkness or daylight.

These boats were rowed from four rower positions, two on port and two on starboard, and they were staggered so as to not be directly across from one another, a design which facilitated precise maneuvering. Strong rowers added increased speed when it was needed, such as for getting to shore ahead of an approaching storm, or for offering the catch for sale before other boats arrived and drove down the day's price by the increase in supply. The four rowers were directed by a helmsman, making five on board, that fifth was most often the crew chief, often the owner. When used for seine net fishing, at least two additional men were customary to work the nets, which brought the boat's number to seven. When the resurrected Jesus appeared on the nearby shore to Peter and others as told in John 21, there were seven men in Peter's boat.

The length of the typical fishing boat was twenty-six feet. If one is a boater, comparisons of length are now running through the mind but, if one is not a boater, several comparisons are helpful. The standard American yellow school bus is thirty-seven feet from front to back bumpers, meaning it's eleven feet longer than a Galilean boat. The four-wheel twenty-seven-foot urban delivery truck, one with its front tires beside the motor housing and its rear tires about eight feet from its rear doors, is only one foot longer than the typical Galilean fishing boat. They were not big boats.

Some modern accounts declare the length and beam of the Galilean boats permitted as many as thirteen to fifteen persons aboard. With that number, there would have been insufficient space for nets and associated equipment, much less for a welcomed catch of fish. That number was most probably the load capacity when a boat was used to ferry passengers as they often did, for boats were used for fishing, transportation of persons and cargo, including loose grain, and occasionally as a floating platform for addressing a multitude, as we know from Scripture. A passenger dedicated boat would be used primarily for passengers and/or cargo instead of for fishing, given the slippery surfaces and odors of a fishing boat. Rembrandt's 1633 *The Storm on the Sea of Galilee* depicts one passenger in fervent prayer, others working the boat, while still others seem to be simply conversing with Jesus, but it is a painting conjured from the artist's knowledge of centuries-later Dutch boats of comparable size.

When fishing, a boat's seine net was kept at its stern, enabling it to be run out by the boat moving forward, worked with a second boat in deep or shallow water, and then in time drawn back in, a strenuous task. Peter and Zebedee's boats worked in tandem. The bottoms of their boats were nearly flat, with minimal keel, those design features and rowers enabling them to work in the shallow water which is a characteristic of the fish-laden typography of this lake. It was a procedure important not only for bringing netted fish into the boats or passing a seine net's four ropes to those waiting on shore to assist in hauling the net and fish within it to the bank and awaiting baskets.

Because these boats were expensive to acquire new, repairing one or buying a repaired one was less costly. Thinking about repairs to a used car, truck or tractor compared to the price of a new one is an apt analogy in our day. Consequently, the specific boat discussed in the next chapter was repaired many times. For any distance other than a short one, it was easier to move persons from village to village by boat than by foot, as it was easier to move goods by boat than by human, donkey, mule, horse, or camel. Their uses for transportation of people, animals, and goods was a source of income for boat owners. We know that Jesus went between shoreline communities sometimes by boat.

The economics of Galilean fishing were not simple, and it was a sometimes profitable enterprise and sometimes not. Owners of boats fished from them with immediate or extended family and, if short-handed, with friends or hired hands. Participants could have been paid in whole or in part from fish caught. Fish markets and processing areas were adjacent to where boats brought their catch ashore and served not only the local population but as early points for distant markets. Fish were gutted and moved quickly for local sale as fresh fish, while others were dried, smoked, salted or pickled for export. Net incomes would rise when the catches were good but also from renting boats to men working in shifts, albeit a crew in a rented boat was competition with its owner and his crew. As a fisherman will acknowledge when pressed, when fishing is good, it is usually underreported to others as only fair, but when it is bad, it is most often truly bad. Prolonged good catches mean better times, but they are seldom sustained for more than a few seasons. Good times are always followed by bad times, the first hoped and worked for and the second dreaded. Whether in good or bad times, the owner's crew usually fished at night during hot months, the owner renting his boat to other crews that then had to fish on other nights or during the day. This division was flipped in cooler months.

Because Jewish fishermen were proscribed from fishing on the Sabbath and fish caught by them on that day were regarded as defiled by that sin, some Jewish owners may have rented out their boats to Gentiles for their fishing on the Sabbath and holy days' nights. It may have been tempting nonetheless to Jewish fishermen hard pressed for income not to fish on Sabbath nights especially because Roman authorities were probably less vigilant because of their knowledge of the proscription, such fishermen motivated by avoiding the tax on fish caught. If fish caught on the Sabbath were regarded as contaminated by the sin, was coin paid for the use of rented boats used on the Sabbath similarly tarnished?

As to the finances of boat ownership, an account in the following chapter posits a boat was stripped and scuttled because its owner had bought a new one and therefore no longer needed that one. That may be unlikely because a repaired boat still had value, and the owner of the new boat could have sold the old one to recover at least some funds to apply toward the cost of the new boat. Someone just entering competition on the water might have bought it, or its planking and other wood could have been carefully removed and used for repair of other boats. For the poor around the sea, and there was no shortage of them, it could have been taken apart and its wood sold or given free as kindling and its nails resold or bartered. None of those scenarios happened in respect to that boat. Instead, it was scuttled, remained under the water line and almost totally under the lakebed's mud for approximately twenty centuries. It is also possible that particular boat for whatever reason could have been intentionally hidden from authorities, hidden quite effectively by its submersion below the water line.

What was the nature of the fishermen known to Jesus? We can surmise they were plain-garbed men of experiential learning from their lives of fishing's knowable yet sometimes inexplicable successes and failures. As orientalist Gustaf Dalman has written, their fishing experience included their deep-seated awareness that "human endeavor alone does not guarantee prosperity." Their shoulders were probably broad, their arms strong, their skin bronzed by the intense sun, their beards unkempt, their fishing tunics old, and their hands calloused. From what we know of them, they had not been men of spiritual sensitivities, a lack demonstrated repeatedly and of which Jesus was sometimes annoyingly well aware. Because we do not know everything about them, we would like to know why he selected each of them for his own reasons; perhaps, he was informed by what John the Baptist may have shared with him as to those known to him.

Many boats taking many fish from the lake would have put heavy pressure on this fishery. Recent discoveries of fourteen first-century fishing harbors confirm that pressure, a not surprising number, for villagers knew a harbor, no matter how small, could enhance the village's economy. As to the volume of fish, if demand was high but fish few, price would go up. Because too many fish caught relative to market demand would have driven prices down, holding pens in the water near the shoreline were constructed of massive smooth cut stones anchored by their own weight to the lake's bottom. These pens had narrow passages between the blocks to assure water circulation, openings wide enough for water to flow but not wide enough for fish to escape. Flat surface stones above the waterline enabled men to walk on them and remove fish by dip nets to an adjacent boat to be taken to shore for sale. I am not aware of such a pen having been built surrounding an underwater spring infusing new fresh water into the lake but, if I had been there then, I would like to believe I would have suggested one for its benefit to the captive fish.

CHAPTER 11

The Boat

What we now know with specificity about Galilean boats came by way of a dramatic saga which began during the last weeks of December 1985. While it unfolded over months and then a second phase over several years, the lifelong hope of two brothers became a reality, and a news story which in short time traveled globally. What was it?

The outline of a partially preserved, meaning also partially decayed, boat was spotted by two adult brothers in recently exposed mud along the Sea of Galilee's northwestern shore. A three-year drought had caused a historically low water level, leaving what had been lake bottom under several feet of water exposed as quickly drying mudflats. The drought had already lowered the lake's surface to such an extent that Mendel Nun, a widely regarded Sea of Galilee expert and amateur archaeologist, was able to identify what remained of fourteen ports from Jesus's time. The boat discovered by the Lufan brothers, Moshe and Luval, was the traditional twenty-six feet in length with a beam of seven-and-a-half feet. More important, and from the outset, it was suspected by its particular design and construction to be the remains of an ancient watercraft.

It was, and in being such a craft it provided a direct link to biblical times.

In the years which followed the discovery, Professor Shelley Wachsmann, Israel's Inspector of Underwater Antiquities from 1976 to 1989 at its Department of Antiquities and Museums, later renamed the Israel Antiquities Authority, wrote and had published several accounts of the finding, recovery, restoration and exhibiting of this boat. His *Understanding The Boat from the Time of Jesus* and his and others' publications, particularly Nun's *The Sea of Galilee and Its Fishermen in the New Testament* and Lea Lofenfeld Winkler and Ramit Frenkel's *The Boat and the Sea of Galilee*, are the bases for the descriptions here of the discovery and restoration of the boat discovered, including in the important context of other boats of that and prior eras. Nun lived, worked from and wrote at Kibbutz Ein Gev on the eastern shore of the lake near the ruins of Hippos, one of the ancient Decapolis (Ten Cities) founded and named during the area's Greek occupation, and he was considered to be "a walking encyclopedia for everything relating to the history, botany, and zoology" of the lake, and Nun's text, photographs and graphic art further detail what he, Wachsmann, and Winkler describe. Wachsmann's begins with information on Galilean seafaring prior to and at the time of the Gospels' accounts following which he discusses the discovered boat, while Nun's provides informative overviews of the nets used in ancient times and the fish caught. Winkler and Frenkel's account is a nearly hour-by-hour recitation of the tense events following the boat's discovery and guarded awareness of its importance. It's nearly impossible to read them without being inspired to visit Galilee and its shoreline villages, related sites and the museum housing this boat amidst artifacts and descriptions of the area and its long history.

It is not my place to capture all of what they researched, wrote, and agreed to be published for the benefits of scholars, pilgrims, fishers, and others but, with this acknowledgment and appreciation of their hard work, we can at least review their highlights for they too have become important insights into the region's history. Readers can purchase each of these books for their captivating details, because each remains available. I implore the reader to read their words and review their photographs and then go to Israel to visit the museum and see this boat and much else. First-hand observation nearly always outweighs written accounts.

The Lufans, members of Kibbutz Ginosar on the western edge of the lake, had long-standing interests and experiences in archaeology encompassing the Roman occupation. Described by Winkler and Frenkel as two fishing brothers whose entire world was more the lake than the land and who followed their hearts, their eyes and ears were always open to what was new for them. They had hoped since childhood to find the remains of an ancient fishing boat, they did, and it went into local lore and history books and travel accounts as their discovery. Their find is amplified by its details.

A military truck traveling in darkness along the shoreline became stuck, its driver unaware of springs in locations along its edge which create deep sucking mud. The driver tried to get unstuck by rocking back and forth, but that worsened the situation as its large tires spun to more than a meter's depth. The Lufan brothers became aware of this occurrence and came near sunrise the next morning to see if the tires had spun out anything of interest. To their joy, they found a bronze coin which they believed to be a poor widow's mite, known also as a lepton, the smallest of Roman era coins at roughly the size of a United States dime. Widow mites had come into use in Judea about a century before Jesus's birth and went out of circulation during the first century AD. When used, a widow's mite declared its holder to be poor, an indication of that weak value being it took eight to buy a single sparrow. Encouraged as to what else might be in the sprayed mud, they got on their knees, dug further with their hands, and found more of these coins. They were authenticated by the kibbutz's archaeologist, Claire Epstein, as having been minted during the 103–76 BC reign of King Alexander Jannaeus. A mite as an object lesson is described by Jesus in Mark 12.

Their day jobs' priorities being what they were, it was a week before the Lufans returned to the site to see what else they might find. The 1983, 1984, and 1985 drought's reduced water levels had exposed compacted mud flats. What they found this time were several nails attached to the surviving upper boards of a sunken boat nearly fully encased in lake bottom mud. They quickly reported their find to the kibbutz's leadership which in turn undertook prompt actions to protect the site in order to preserve from curious hands whatever remained of the boat. The Antiquities Authority was notified immediately with a four-word message: "a shipwreck—possible ancient." There was no need for additional words to request the Authority send experts right away, for with exciting thoughts in their own minds, they did.

Wachsmann, Kurt Raveh, and several others, perhaps the brothers' relatives and the Authority's conservator Orna Cohen, joined the brothers and members of the kibbutz to see what the outline of the boat might yield. While its exposed upper inches remained water-logged, they saw that the lower hull had been preserved by the far less oxygenated mud, for most of the surviving section of the boat was not as water-logged as it was mud-logged. By examining its uppermost hull strake, those not familiar with boats would refer to that strake as a sideboard, and seeing that one board was joined to another by pegged mortise and tenon joints, they knew immediately it was an ancient craft. Its "hull first" assembly made it unlike the "ribs first" assemblies which would follow for centuries. A later precise timeframe would confirm within which hundred years the trees for it had grown before being cut for use in its wood work.

How can one not be deeply moved by Wachsmann's paragraph following his realization that they had indeed uncovered a very special boat?

> In our excitement, we barely noticed that it had begun to rain. Soon torrents of water descended upon us as we all piled into my jeep. The cloudburst was short-lived, stopping as suddenly as it had started, but it left behind a magnificent double-rainbow cascading into the Sea of Galilee—as if we had ordered it from Central Casting.

Such an order had not been needed. There are photographs in *Understanding The Boat* and *The Boat and the Sea of Galilee* of the distinct double-rainbow beyond them as it touched the sea's surface. When I first saw these photographs, chill bumps ran across my shoulders as that photographed sky seemed to me to have said, "Job well done" and perhaps "at long last" or as Michael Hesemann described it, "the floodgates of heaven were opened." Hesemann is a German archaeologist widely respected for his knowledge of Galilee and its sea.

The rainfall which came in the following days was the heaviest in three years and created an urgency to move the boat to shore. As described by these authors, the excavation of the boat required a sequence of immediate tasks to be saved from "desiccation and disintegration," Hesemann's apt description. The tasks were to remove the mud and gravel from it, remove all debris from the area immediately surrounding it, study, photo and otherwise record everything while still in place, and then remove the hull for tedious conservation and restoration and eventual display. The boat and descriptions of it and these events are now on display at the Beit Yigal Allon Museum not far from where it was discovered and had much, if not most or all, of its floating life two millennia before its discovery. Further, these publications are generally available in Israeli and other bookstores and, if you cannot find them there, online.

With the prospect of exhibiting it several years later, complicated restoration had to begin immediately to avoid feared deterioration from exposure to air. A project operations chart was devised in this context, as Winkler and Frenkel point out, in that no group anywhere had ever discovered a wooden boat that had been buried in fresh water for two thousand years give or take a few decades. In a hush-but-rush manor the first steps were taken, for the long wished winter rains had come and begun raising the water level at the same time news about the boat was spreading. The boat was extracted from the lake in mid to late February 1986. The mud had indeed preserved much of the wooden hull and the iron nails reinforcing its joints.

The Antiquities Authority's leadership knew it needed a prompt but independent verification of its conclusion on the boat's provenance before an erroneous or speculative news account was published locally and went widespread. Much was at stake in authenticating and adding to that conclusion. Jumping too quickly to what archaeological findings said about the past, which then turned out to be either wrong or not sufficiently provable, had plagued the Holy Land for centuries, even more so after the 1948 establishment of modern Israel had expanded both professional archaeological digs and the by-products of government and commercial excavations for reconstructions or new constructions of buildings. The latter two categories of the three had become commonplace as Israel gained its economic footing following 1948 and new buildings grew in communities and arid lands became irrigated farmlands, excavators and plows routinely uncovering ancient artifacts. The Authority knew the boat was ancient, but its age alone was only one answer among others needed to satisfy anticipated demands for verified answers.

These concerns led the Israelis to the world's then pre-eminent authority in underwater archaeology and ancient boat construction, but he was far away from their site. He was J. Richard Steffy, professor of Nautical Archaeology at Texas A&M University in College Station, a pioneering instructor and university educator in this learn-by-experience area of scholarship undertaken through their collaborating Institute on Nautical Archaeology. College Station is about an hour and a half drive northwest of Houston's international airport from which Steffy's 7,000-mile flights to Israel began. He had been an electrical contractor until he was forty-eight, an occupation and its job security set aside to pursue his passion for studying shipwrecks. Only thirteen years after his pivotal choice he was named a MacArthur Fellow at the John D. and Catherine T. MacArthur Foundation in recognition of his transformative scholarship and descriptions of viable methodologies in nautical archaeology. This prestigious fellowship and the funds which accompanied it provided, in his words, "both time and funding" to complete his 1994 *Wooden Ship Building and the Interpretation of Shipwrecks,* a 314-page instructional guide on, again his words, "the most marvelous structures ever built by humankind—wooden ships and boats." The institute's legacy includes global recognition of his and its expertise in assisting the discovery, identification, study, and thoughtful publicizing of archaeological sites to foster additional support for a once-overlooked field of history and science and, in some cases, the recovery in whole or part and preservation and exhibition in museums of some of the vessels.

When I reviewed the beginning-to-end timeline of the boat's discovery, restoration and museum display, it took me several readings to appreciate how the total process had remarkably few stumbling blocks. Wachsmann's *Understanding The Boat,* as well as Winkler and Frenkel's, Hesseman's and others' accounts, persuaded me that expected government and organizational bureaucracy, call it red tape, road blocks or high hurdles, took a rare back seat on this project. It was as if an unseen hand was orchestrating its intricacies. Enter at nearly the outset of this authentication process the United States' ambassador to Israel, Thomas Pickering. What a coincidence that was, for he was not only a highly capable career diplomat but also a scholar of the region's many complexities, a man with long-held archaeological interests, and a friend too of a number of my acquaintances in Washington.

Professor Steffy had a narrow window of time between previously scheduled commitments to come to Galilee to inspect the boat and tender an expert opinion. What could have been many government prerequisites were cut through with Ambassador Pickering's astute guidance. Steffy was in the air nearly immediately after receiving the Authority's request to travel to the site of the boat. What he brought to this opportunity and its challenges was beyond strict nautical archaeological scholarship. It generated morale-building excitement around the notion that back-breaking work can be well-directed and professionally and personally rewarding. His arrival was replete with the potential for that excitement, but it was nonetheless a nervous set of moments. He knew everything about his field of study and could, in the words of Winkler and Frenkel, read ancient wood and boat design like a newspaper. When he arrived on the mudflat, the excavation team members held their collective breath to await his conclusions.

At the end of his preliminary examination, he told them this was indeed an ancient boat from somewhere in the second century BC to at least the Roman occupation. He did not tell them his first impression by using a university professor's erudite or technical language, instead saying simply "Yup, it's an old boat." Then he added the details on how he had come to that conclusion. A collective sigh of relief arose and the project's momentum accelerated, but it was not without important clarifications. He surprised them with his judgment that the boat had been built for sailing, whatever its actual use or uses were two thousand years ago. How had he come swiftly to such a conclusion? From examining the exposed sideboards. If it had been built for the Mediterranean Sea's waters or for heavy cargo or passenger work on this inland sea, the sideboard's thickness would have been three to four inches. In contrast, this boat's sideboards were slightly less than an inch, meaning among other characteristics that it weighed far less and was more maneuverable but theoretically less durable. It's survival for two thousand years showed otherwise as to that durability, for it had been strengthened to offset the potential weakness of thin sideboards, an indication itself that it was used for heavier tasks than sailing. How so?

He described how the nail patterns showed the boat had been finished or later repaired by someone less knowledgeable at boat building than a boat-wright would have been. Maybe it was available because someone who had commissioned its building ran short of the funds required to pay the boat-wright to finish the project? Maybe it was because someone who needed the boat for a purpose inconsistent with a boat already under construction but was immediately available for purchase if modified by mutual agreement? Maybe it was a carpenter who knew much about woods and nails but little about the proper use of nails in a boat's construction? Maybe it was someone who sought some years after its construction to strengthen it after the wear and tear of earlier years? Whoever drove the nails into its wood illustrated their uncertainty by using more nails than a boat-wright would have used. The tactic seemed to be if one nail at a joint was a good thing, two nails were a doubly good thing. There were a number of such places in the boat at which those listening to his explanation were standing or squatting.

The mud's anaerobic state had inhibited bacteria's normal course of destroying woods and water-born oxygen's normal course of rusting nails. *National Geographic*'s December 2017 account concluded the project to remove this boat from the seabed, which normally would have taken months of planning and labor, was completed in eleven or twelve days and nights. Why that "or"? Maybe because not everyone recalls that each day is surrounded by two nights and each night by two days. Maybe also that nightfall to nightfall is a more meaningful calculation in the region's dominant Jewish culture than our midnight to midnight. Maybe even more so, a year in the Hebrew calendar can be 353, 354, 355, 383, 384, or 385 days long and, while regular common years have twelve months with a total of 354 days, leap years have thirteen months and are 384 days long. In a world of such a complex calendar system, why get too precise over whether it was eleven or twelve days?

As the boat was freed from the mud, it was encased within a mantle of fiberglass and an insulating polyurethane glycol (PEG) foam and floated to shore. It was further cleaned, refloated in a fresh water holding tank in which tilapia and pet store-like goldfish were introduced to eat the worms, parasites and algae which emerged from it in its pool of fresh water. The latter was a tactic suggested by co-discoverer Moshe Lufan. That stage completed, the boat was refloated in a pool of sixty tons of preservative to prevent further deterioration of the remaining wood. One account reports six years of this step and another ten, but perhaps six was the length of one of the two treatments within a ten-year period. That set out, other accounts report the boat's time in the conservation tank phase was fourteen years, which seems unlikely since it was removed from its mud encasement in 1986 and was already available for public display at the Vatican prior to 2000.

A display in Rome did not occur for reasons of high risks in shipment of such a fragile relic and the agreed-upon need for more pilgrims traveling to the Holy Land in that Jubilee year than to Rome. Thought out politely but accurately, Rome could wait for future opportunities to display the craft, but another idea emerged. Rome would not receive the original boat. Instead, it received in October 2023 a precise reproduction of it, built mostly with cedar by the Aponte family builders of wooden boats. Known there as "la barca di tutti," "the ship of all," colloquially, everyone's boat, it was installed by them, received and blessed by Pope Francis, and placed permanently near the entrance of the Vatican Museums. What a visual and what a location to highlight Jesus's connection to fishermen, fishing and fish.

A metal shed was built over the pool area to protect it and earn income by way of admissions to cover some of the costs of its restoration. Now resting on a stainless steel frame surrounded by temperature- and moisture-controlled air, special lighting, and straight forward descriptions of the discovery and restoration process, the boat is now the centerpiece of the Beit Yigal Allon

Museum near where it was discovered. The Carbon-14 analyses of the wood samples removed from the boat were undertaken by Israel's multidisciplinary Weizman Institute of Science in Rehovot which determined that the woods were cut on average in 40 BC, plus or minus eighty years.

Additional determinations placed the provenance of the boat, a ceramic pot, a fisherman's lamp and nails of various designs found with the boat to the same decades of those woods. With these confirmations, world attention to the boat grew, as did interests in this inland sea in Galilee, its fishermen and its fish. Those interests were not limited to Jews and Christians, but they were more proportional to them. Interest grew as well among archaeologists, especially nautical archaeologists. Hesemann sets out a case for the boat's history tied to the naval battle of Migdal in 67 AD and associated with Flavius Josephus, and that could be true, but its earlier history encompasses the years Jesus had frequent uses of boats on the lake, this speculation being its only presently known tie to him.

I wondered myself if it might have been Peter's boat, sunk to be hidden by Jesus's followers in order to hide it from Temple or Roman authorities suspected by them of having intentions to destroy it because of that association, but that's because I know from a half-century of professional experience in public affairs that self-interested political behavior is often defensive, protective and destructive.

If Peter and his crew feared, in the wake of Jesus's stacked trial against him and crucifixion, that Roman and/or Temple authorities might seek to destroy Peter's boat, they could have sunk it near the shoreline by filling it with heavy lake bottom sand and mud. It may have been done quickly.

Ella Werker at Hebrew University in Jerusalem identified the wood samples taken from the recovered boat's hull. While the planking was mainly cedar and its frames were oak, the boat, including many repairs to it, consisted of ten additional woods: Aleppo pine, Atlantic terebinth, carob, hawthorn, laurel, plane, redbud, sidder, sycamore, and willow. The only wood not native to the Galilean area was the sturdy and aromatic cedar which came from the direction of Lebanon, whose modern national flag bears a likeness of a cedar tree in representation of the famed Cedars of Lebanon. Wachsmann's account reports trees of each of these woods are now planted on the north side of the roadway leading to the museum, quite a thoughtful landscape measure.

Like other discussions associated with religion, debates about this boat were inevitable. Boats such as this one are mentioned fifty times in the Gospels. Even though there were no specific facts linking this boat directly with Jesus or his fishermen, some persons began referring to it as the Jesus boat, perhaps because they hoped he had preached from it or directed his disciples on how to net fish from it.

The kibbutz's leaders knew they had a boat of much historic value, and they responded with respect, urgency, and some of the funds required. It became the center piece of the museum designed, built, owned and operated by it. I have been to it twice, once when it was open and there was much time to adsorb the exhibit's accounts and discuss it with curators, and several years later less than five minutes after it had closed for the day in successful defiance of my fervent pleas to reopen "for just five minutes." Brian Waidmann, a longtime friend and professional acquaintance, and I were on a pilgrimage. Carol Ann Bernheim was our licensed guide for our days in Galilee and asked if we wished to stop less than two miles from the boat museum to take a brief walk into Wadi Hamam. *Wadi* is Arabic for a ravine or small valley, and this wadi was off the roadway we were traveling as she posed that question.

It is a segment of the pathway between Nazareth and the Sea of Galilee at the time of Jesus and long before and long after. During Jesus's time Wadi Hamam was populated with several settlements of public buildings, residences, granaries and olive-oil presses, and more. All appear to have been destroyed by the Romans in the second century AD, perhaps as retribution for the Bar Kokhba Jewish revolt against the Romans.

Archeological works underway in the wadi will continue to inform those who walk it. It drains the volcanic plateau of Hattin and has abundant but seasonal fresh water springs which must have been welcomed in those centuries but, even in ancient times as now, were drained for irrigation purposes. In the years before Jesus walked through it, Jews adhering faithfully to their law but regarded by Romans and their allies as outlaws were smoked out of its caves by Herod's soldiers hanging in cages at their entrances. In later years Flavius Josephus fortified its cave of Arbela against Roman forces intent on seizing the wadi because it was a route used by Jewish rebels. It is now a section of the Jesus Trail between those endpoints, it being a forty-plus mile winding hiking trail from central Nazareth to the lake. If walking is a preferred recreation or a form of pilgrimage more akin to pilgrimages of old, or both, Israel has 6,000-plus miles of religious, otherwise historic, nature-focused, and other trails.

This area is overlooked by Mount Arbel from whose high cliffs much of the sea and this stretch of the Great Rift Valley's topography can be seen in near awe. As an imprecise merging of separate though related geological rift and fault systems, this valley runs southward nearly 5,000 miles down most of the length of East Africa to the distant Zambezi River in Mozambique and northward to the Beqaa Valley in Lebanon. Whether by photographs, video or recall, an observer beholds this view from Mount Arbel more than merely seeing it, for the view is magnificent.

It and Wadi Hamam are near the Horns of Hattin, two extremities of an extinct volcano. As the field of the Battle of the Horns of Hattin it is the site of one of Christian Crusaders greatest defeats. Here in July 1187, An-Nasir Salah ad-Din Yusuf ibn Ayyub, shortened to Salah ad-Din and often contracted further to Saladin, and his 40,000 men on foot aided by 12,000 mounted cavalries killed or captured the vast majority of a large force of culturally, politically and militarily divided crusaders. Of Kurdish ethnicity, Saladin unified Sunni Islam from Upper Mesopotamia through Syria and Egypt and other parts of Asia Minor to Yemen. This victory assured Muslims would be the eminent power in the Holy Land for nearly 800 years, a nearly immediate consequence of which was the surrender to him of Christian-held Jerusalem. A film depiction of Saladin, this battle and its contexts and consequences, the 2005 movie *Kingdom of Heaven*, starring Orlando Bloom, Jeremy Irons, Eva Green, Ghassan Massoud, and Liam Neesen, is a portrayal well worth watching. On my occasion with Waidmann and Bernheim, we sped past one of several water holes made historic by this battle and past much of the battlefield, causing me to recall I had previously visited Saladin's tomb at the northwest corner of the fabled Umayyad Mosque in the Syrian capital city of Damascus. As for this moment, how prescient on Bernheim's part that we stopped at Wadi Hamam, though I did not recognize its significance in the life of Jesus until I was researching the area above the sea's northwestern shore and communities for these pages. In hindsight, that short time connected important dots for me.

Visiting the Beit Yigal Allon Museum is an informing experience of boats and fishing during Jesus's, Peter's, and other fishing apostles' lifetimes. It can be a spiritual experience even without the answers some seek as to the boat's provenance. We should be deeply grateful to the kibbutz's leadership for what they did in preserving and exhibiting the boat and what its current leadership is doing in their footsteps. The museum has been expanded since I first visited it, and visitors to it can now take a nearby boat out onto the lake's waters. When there, I ask myself how many who walk its paths or take the boat excursion know the range of history associated with this stretch of this inland sea and its nearby shoreline. Jesus, Peter, and their fishermen? Yes, of course. The village of Magdala about a mile south and its Mary? Most probably. Roman emperors Vespasian and Titus? Maybe. The Herods? Weren't they down in Jerusalem? The slaughter of many hundreds of men, women, and children in their Galilean boats? Very few. Flavius Josephus's roles in the latter? Quite doubtful.

Visiting the ruins in Magdala and in any other ancient community in modern Israel warrants thoughtful reflection on the lives and roles of the women of the Bible. While its books were carried in oral accounts and later reduced to writings by men and are mostly about men, women were not overlooked, for nearly 300 are set forth by their names in the Old and New Testaments, and more than twenty stand out as significant, beginning with Eve whether corporeal or a composite reference and continuing through Sarah the mother of the Jewish nation; Rebekah, the wife of Issac: Rachel, the wife of Jacob and mother of Joseph; Miriam the sister of Moses; the influential judge Deborah; Delilah, the influencer of Samson; Ruth, a virtuous ancestor of Jesus; Hannah, the mother of the prophet Samuel; Bathsheba, the wife of David and queen mother of King Solomon; Jezebel, queen of Israel; Esther, the influential Persian queen; Elizabeth, the mother of John the Baptist; Mary, the mother of Jesus; Martha, the sister of Lazarus; Mary of Bethany, a follower of Jesus; and Mary Magdalene. As in a funnel of history, they preceded over many centuries of Jewish history the coming and life of Jesus in which some had critical roles. The disparities in the numbers of all men and women, as well as significant men and women of the Bible, its authorship by men, and only men among those whom Jesus first called, should not obscure a certainty of his teaching: that each man and each woman are required to follow the laws of their faith, including the Law of Moses and Jesus's summary commandment to love one another, which means total forgiveness of others' transgressions, and each will be judged accordingly on that basis.

Unearthed in the Magdala excavations are the ruins of a synagogue from the time in which Jesus taught. Its now-named Magdala Stone, a massive altar-like stone with bold carvings not only depicts sacred elements of the Second Temple in Jerusalem but is also the oldest known sculptural depiction of the Temple-Menorah. A second, smaller and therefore probably earlier Torah stone was also located in the synagogue. This discovery ended a long-standing denial of the existence of synagogues in Galilee in Jesus's time, even despite the centurion-built one in Capernaum upon which foundations the White Synagogue was built in the fourth century. This blanket denial reflected a widely held view that Galileans were an impoverished and impious assortment unattached from the center of Israel's religious sites and authorities in Jerusalem. It's not dissimilar from attitudes in our modern era by which those living in centers of governmental and financial power regard those not living there as provincial.

At the risk of repetition and if you have not already done so, after visiting Beit Yigal Allon Museum, turn north and travel several miles to Tabgha and its Church and Rock of the Primacy of Peter, its shortened name being St. Peter's Primacy, the traditional site at which Jesus commanded his fishermen to catch a miraculous number of fish and at which Jesus had a frank discussion with Peter to re-establish in the eyes of the disciples that he was first among them. Then, travel several miles further north of the museum to Capernaum to visit the White Synagogue and the Franciscan Orders' Pilgrimage Church of St. Peter and Peter's house around which it is.

It's somewhat between difficult and not easy to walk along the Sea of Galilee's shoreline in these areas, for there are obstructions which require a walker's attention. I walk around outcroppings and shrubbery and avoid man-made obstructions of centuries past and present. I gaze out over the lake, seeing white tops if the wind is up, and I listen to its waves gently washing the stones at their shared edge, and I feel welcomed breezes. As Michael Hesemann sets out in his *Jesus of Nazareth*, "for a moment present and past blend together, time stands still" and as Michael Gray captures in his *Sacred Places* regarding "the transformative powers of sacred sites" and their "presence of the miraculous," there is indeed an inner peace in being aware of what occurred from the miraculous to the terrifying within the range of one's eyesight here, knowing particularly that Jesus had walked these paths, alone from time to time. Somewhat strangely, it is inescapable in such a setting not to consider how opposing forces may also in the end be complementary, as they come to mind in thinking of Judaism's survival in its differing manifestations and the outgrowth of Christianity, each from their first-century AD crises.

CHAPTER 12

Peter's Fish

Galilean fish have a central role in the life of Jesus for without them there would have been no Galilean fishermen to serve as the innermost core of his disciples. Fishing was important to the livelihoods of those whom he drew first to his mission. Catching, processing, and marketing fish constituted significant commercial undertakings in their day, important enough economically for them to have been heavily regulated by government, primarily through multiple levels of taxes, and to have harbors and adjacent communities centered on fishing, and economic circumstance which continued into the modern era. The Galilean Sea's fish population presently consists of a recently estimated twenty-seven species, nineteen or twenty of which are native and still among the species netted by Jesus's fishermen, but only several species were then and remain now of commercial value.

For centuries before Jesus and his fishermen, the walled Jerusalem had a Fish Gate through which fish brought from Joppa and elsewhere on the Mediterranean coastline and the Sea of Galilee were brought to its fish market, for fish were an important food.

Fish as food were subject to Jewish culinary laws. Pelagic fish, those living primarily in the upper levels of water columns, were kosher, while bottom feeders were prohibited by this cultural regulatory mechanism and had commercial value only by sale to Gentiles. By examples, the fabled St. Peter's fish, which is a tilapia, was kosher, but a catfish was not. For the Roman, Greek, and nomadic populations living at or near the lake, the Jewish distinction between edible and inedible was irrelevant, so they bought and ate as they pleased. Kosher fish had their own markets while other fish had other markets. In the modern era, the Israeli government stocks the lake to sustain the annual catch of kosher fish.

An abundance of the sea's tilapia in any particular fishing ground depended in large measure on the season of the year. In cooler weather, the broad northern shore of the lake seemed favored by tilapia and in that respect Masterman reported that the richest fishing ground was close to Bethsaida, this phenomenon authenticating the town's name as "house of fishing." In warmer weather, the marshy delta of the Jordan seemed favored. Boats and their nets followed the fish across a spectrum of fishers' knowledge from years of experience to accounts heard of yesterday's catches and failures and, in this respect, it mirrors nearly all forms of fishing. The currency of hearsay is given much attention.

Tilapia and perhaps other fish appear on menus throughout the region as St. Peter's Fish or Peter's Fish. Managers of eateries may decide which name to use based on their own religious faith or that suspected by them to be the faith of most of their customers. I use St. Peter's Fish in my own references while there in order to stress that at least one fisherman in the annals of history was a saint.

CHAPTER 13

How Do Jesus's Teachings Relate to Us?

Jesus's teachings give guidance to each of us, it being our decision how to respond to them, said precisely, each of us. Together, the teachings pose questions. What have we learned from our past? How can we use that learning to shape our present and future? How will those answers motivate us to make decisions important to ourselves and through ourselves to others? In both the short and long runs, only each of us, not professional counselors, family members or friends, should make the decisions crucial to your life. Ownership of our decisions is crucial to our acceptance of them.

Few observations capture this point as persuasively in its humanity, theology and sheer logic as a recent posting, one on Ruvim Borishkevich's "I love to talk about Jesus" platform:

> If getting into heaven was the only goal for a Christian, God would've taken your life the moment you accepted Christ. However, He didn't because the

> goal of Christianity is to be the hands and feet of Jesus. That's actually why you're called "the body of Christ." We're called to be Jesus to the people around us. That's the only way the world will ever experience God's love. If heaven is your only motivation, you're living in selfishness, not love.

Let's explore his point.

The present can be unsettling because the prospect of tomorrows different from yesterdays can be outside one's comfort zone. As a matter of fact, it often is. That's unfortunate, because it blocks the possibility that a new zone can emerge with greater, perhaps far greater, comfort than the one which receded. Resolving issues works that way. Being more comfortable with a known past than an unknown future leaves one in a direction constrained by incomplete or even inaccurate facts and their contexts.

What a person knows about anything is rarely everything of importance there is to know about it. A past encompasses life begun and continued in the transformative effects of childhood's nuclear and extended families, neighbors and neighborhoods, education in classrooms and school yards, career and other workplace experiences, places of worship, communities of volunteers, friends and foes, together everything and everyone. Yet, the totality of breadth and depth surrounding you means that you know only part of how those facts and circumstances relate to your life and a specific focus later recalled. Understanding more is important and understanding far more is essential to a more complete understanding of one's own self.

I was surprised in nearly all of the categories of life experiences when I spent more than three years doing research for what became my *Families: Where We Each Begin*. I benefitted the most from persons in and out of my family observing to me "That's not quite right" however they would phrase that, and then their sharing their additional information and impressions with me. It was a process which considerably expanded my knowledge of myself. Some observations were just nuances, but many were descriptions of facts and circumstances of major significance of which I had had no knowledge.

Since what you intend at the end of a process of self-awareness is not required to be wholly formed at the outset, why be reluctant about beginning that process? The intention required to start and stay the course will be made easier by knowing the journey will take the passage of time for new habits of thinking and doing to overtake and surpass old ones. Internalizing the words of Jesus, "Be not afraid," bolstered me, for I needed the perspective, encouragement and shelter it created, a safe harbor in a life of often rough seas. Recognizing that a step at a time committed me only to considering the next step helped me undertake a longer journey.

New answers emerged more readily *for me* because I had accepted the divine nature of Jesus, thereby the truth of his wisdom as I understood it. While his words focus on how the present exists within a continuum, they also focus on the daily paths which lead first to self-awareness and then to reckonings with others. Some do not regard Jesus as divine, rather as a teacher of a cohesive set of high ethical values for persons to follow, an historic person on a level of major influence comparable to the world's other principal religious faiths. That conclusion might be understandable if made in respect only to his teaching, but his words authenticate him only in part.

What else authenticates him is his exercise of God-like powers: the miraculous healing of persons afflicted with debilitating medical infirmities—restoring the dead to life as well as restoring eyesight and uses of limbs, ending other physiological and neurological illnesses. So, too, the changing of physical properties—calming wind and sea, changing water into wine, enormous multiplication of loaves and fishes, walking on water, each of which was the exercise of God-like power witnessed by persons ranging from a few to thousands and described credibly in contemporaneous accounts. Through his words he demonstrated wisdom, but through his miracles he demonstrated divinity. As man, he was of this world, but in his exercise of divine power, he was also of another world, although in both natures he sought to improve the internal and external lives of those who were of this world.

There is another dimension to what distinguishes the Abrahamic faiths from other religions, and it is of fundamental significance to our understanding of them. It is that Judaism and Christianity are revealed religions, ones based on divine revelation from God rather than from reasoning alone. God revealed to humankind, specifically through the Hebrews a moral order based on ten precisely stated commandments, the bilateral agreement of them constituting a covenant by which they agreed to adhere to them in exchange for their having been chosen by him in all its dimensions. This was followed centuries later by God sending Jesus in human form to articulate, stress and strive toward a broad acceptance of those commandments in the Hebrew and other nations' persons' daily lives, that is, by their understanding of God's love for them should be and best is reflected in their love for one another. How did these two events relate?

Scripture in the Pentateuch followed the receipt of the Ten Commandments and added additional rules for living, and the books of the Hebrew Bible following the Pentateuch added still others. After a protracted period in which God witnessed Hebrews obeying and other Hebrews not obeying the first ten, God oversaw the birth into their number of one in which the powers of God would be manifested through such profound events as miraculous conception, transfiguration, resurrection, and ascension, the additional directive to love one another as a much more assured means by which to understand and obey all the tenets. Jesus was the proclaimer of this as well as the articulator of the rewards and penalties for failure to abide by them.

Jesus set out a view of the Judaism into which he was born and as to which he and events following his crucifixion and resurrection had consequences. Some of that view was internalized into the Christianity which emerged. Despite powerful resistances, it survived and expanded through the personal courage and labors of the original disciples known to us by name and unknown to us in the decades which grew into the early and later centuries. They were imbued with individual and shared hopes even though often permeated with fears, which when bolstered by their beliefs in Jesus were accepted or overcome.

His teachings added to the Judaic code of personal conduct, the Ten Commandments, a new requirement, that of deepest love, not as an abstraction but rather as an inspiration, aspiration, and action. If followed in enlarging number of persons, they would cause changes to emerge by expanding the effects of this addition from individuals to families, families to neighbors, neighbors to communities and, when joined by others acting similarly, even larger settings. The peace of which Jesus spoke was not the peace between nations as a consequence of diplomatic negotiations or political and/or military victories, but rather the inner peace arising from the love of one another set into the framework of the commandments. This peace was to rise from inner reflections and move to conduct in words and deeds, in time becoming a new personal attitude and gradually a new personal habit, those of a few joining others to become similar habits of the many. It is today the world's largest religion.

Jesus's declaration that love of one another should be the guiding force between persons was not meant as a superlative of the word like, it being an emotional affection, a gratifying enjoyment. When we commonly say we love something we usually mean we like it a lot and for its pleasure's sake. In those instances, we let experienced-derived emotions screen the deeper meaning of love. Again, what else is there to the love of which he spoke? Sincerity. We know that Jesus spoke some Greek for a Greek population existed in his Galilee, and we find his use of Greek words, such as hypocrite, in biblical accounts of his teaching. The love of which he speaks to us is captured in the Greek word *agape* [äˈgäˌpā, ˈagəpā] and in modern usage [əˈgāp, Uh-GAH-pay], a selfless, sacrificial, unconditional love. It is steadfast, unwavering, and uniting, a place between God's love for us received from one direction, accepted and internalized, and its imparting to other persons in a followed-on direction. The lay theologian C.S. Lewis captured that latter point when he wrote: "Love is unselfishly choosing for another's highest good," and another commentator defined it as "a heartfelt response to a mindful choice, resulting in a commitment to care about others and producing actions to meet their needs."

The emotional and habitual barriers to a gradual or immediate transition to love in its many dimensions are the resentment, anger, hostility, downright hate we may feel toward those that have wronged us and our get-even attitude, the desired revenge we too often feel and then seek, sometimes even in public spaces, in order to humiliate and destroy, sometimes financially. We can do this no matter how distant in time or remoteness the transgression against us. Jesus's message to us is not a naively fantasized utopianism but rather a framework to reduce harm in ways which are intended to give rise to more civility toward one another. I am so guilty of these thoughts and acts.

Over time I worked out one response which enabled me to move beyond resentment, anger, hostility, even hate, one which neutralized in varying degrees my otherwise negative reactions. Jesus said it (Mark 23:34) from the cross: "Father, forgive them, for they know not what they do." I cannot tell you how quickly one can move from resentment, anger, hostility, even hate than by saying to yourself "Father, forgive them, for they know not what they do." Recall these words, and say them within your mind the next time you need them. It wipes my slate clean as to the matter, so I can refocus, and does so without confrontation. While it may seem arrogant, it is actually quite the opposite, for it is an effective way of turning the other cheek, and that's a way of moving on.

Jesus's unconditional love may be the most difficult to achieve because we doubt ourselves worthy of its proffer, but it is not that difficult if we are of the right mind in both following the commandments and extending the deepest love to others. It will be accomplished more readily by abandoning at the outset any expectation of love returned at the level offered, for his love does not rest on a quid pro quo. A Christian's inner guide must be the continued offer of love, for in giving love at this depth and not expecting its return at this depth liberates us from often heavy emotional burdens. The lack of his level of love imprisons us in animosities and expectations which will seldom, perhaps never, be overcome or fulfilled.

We liberate our own life by freeing it from others control of it through their intentional or unintentional actions or inactions on one hand and from our own speculations of what we believe their attitudes toward us are or may be on the other. A desire for an equivalent or any other response may limit our continued offer of love to the other person. In thinking and acting in this way we obey the commandments in recognition they are expressions of deep love from God to be expressed in turn by us to our parents, our spouses, our neighbors. This love actualizes Jesus's words on how many times, "seventy times seven" he said to Peter, we are to forgive another, no matter how difficult that may be.

Is a concise, yet coherent and credible, summary of these observations possible? Yes, and it came to me from a friend with whom I worked for decades in addressing the delivery of medical services to the indignant of East Africa, a person whose experientially, intellectually and spiritually acquired knowledge of Christianity is deep enough to be hostile to the sinners who lead themselves and others astray but still deep enough to encourage them to a different life by his love of them. Paraphrasing, he implores each of us to love unconditionally, serve God's purposes rather than our own, humble our self, give to others without seeking a return, empower others rather than controlling them, show mercy rather than judgment or revenge, seek justice and freedom for all persons, encourage and motivate others rather than discourage them, spread hope and joy, and believe and live in faith.

At nearly the same time he shared them with me and others, my smart phone displayed for me two similar observations from two authors both of which were labeled Unknown: "It took me a long time to understand what it means to forgive someone. But after a lot of soul searching, I realized that forgiveness is not about accepting or excusing their behavior. It's about letting it go and preventing their behavior from destroying my heart" written with the same conclusion and guidance in mind of another's "I never knew how strong I was until I had to forgive someone who wasn't sorry, and accept an apology I never received."

A Postscript

You may think this postscript is a disguised preface more appropriate as an introduction. In a way it is, for it does set out how this book was generated and then developed. Its most substantive content needed to be the reader's immediate focus, so those chapters came first. Their focus is the content suggested by the title and cover which caused you to obtain it for yourself, someone else or both. What does this now postscript set out which would have been appropriate for an introduction?

I considered, researched, and wrote these pages with initial trepidation for its subject matters were and remain deeply felt by me while knowing not a one of them found me to be an expert. I came to recognize that awareness as a blessing because it meant I was not locked in by either others' premises and conclusions or even my own. I knew I had to avoid miscues in research and mistakes in writing a book simultaneously simple and complex. The most obvious risk was assuring the accuracy of the names of places, persons, and titles, and dates relative to each, citations of chapters and verses of Scripture, and references to resources, but I knew those challenges would be addressed by repeated verifications. So too were the risks of misstatements of contexts, circumstances or conclusions as reflecting broad consensus when one or more might be only a majority, or even a strongly held minority, opinion. To reduce further these risks, the draft manuscript was reviewed by persons with knowledge greater than mine, and their comments caused revisions to the text. While we should never forget there are few disciplines more fraught with lack of agreement than biblical scholarship, viewpoints will continue to be received and weighed and some incorporated into a follow-on edition should commentators' interests warrant such an edition.

You may have known all, most, more, little, or nothing of the biblical accounts of Jesus and his fishermen, but your level of knowledge was a starting point from which to read these pages and reflect on them. No matter at which level you were, chances are you did not know in depth how much knowledge gained *after* Jesus's life connected us with original accounts of it. The Gospels and the books of the New Testament which followed them in time and placement had end points near the respective times of their writings, but Christianity continued to grow for another twenty centuries.

Aided by modern technologies, much additional and highly relevant knowledge has been gained, and much of it confirmed what was known or suspected from ancient written accounts and other evidence, including archaeological. The latter is a discipline now far beyond pick and shovel, trawl and screen, one truly benefiting from high-tech analyses of bones, ceramics, fibers, metals, terrains, woods, even pollens, and interactions connecting them. Combined, the old and the new scholarships give us understandings beyond our recalls from reading or listening to Scripture and looking at centuries of artists' depictions in mosaics and marbles and on walls, boards and canvases. Consequently, a fuller account of Jesus and his times was able to be set out in these pages, an exciting connection of our present with the past, one full of adventure, suspense and deeper understandings. It was a matter of connecting facts in ways unconnected or seldom connected before recent verifications made such findings and connections possible. While some were quite ordinary tasks, there were also new awarenesses for me, and more than one caused goose bumps to run across my shoulders.

News of Jesus and his fishermen began to spread during the days of their fishing, walking Galilean and other pathways, sitting at common table, worshipping in synagogues, and gathering with others on hillsides and seashores. Their years were a difficult time for Galilean and Judean Jews, for a tense Roman occupation of their lands followed a Greek cultural presence after Alexander the Great's relatively peaceful entry in the fourth century AD. The earliest accounts attest to the ordinary and extraordinary lives set out in the Gospels and other early writings. Together, the old and the new encompassed two thousand years of commentary on the emergence and growth of Christianity from its foundations. The earliest years were followed by the Roman destruction of Jerusalem's Second Temple, a harsh subjugation of Judea and Galilee and the forceful dispersal of many, if not most, Jews from their ancestral homeland. That was followed over a long stretch of history by survivals, successive calamities, and re-growths.

In preparing these pages I reread accounts found in the Gospels and other books of the New Testament, which brought me back to rereading accounts from the Old Testaments at set forth in Hebrew texts translated into English. That included Jewish commentaries on Christian translations of both the Old and New Testament. I moved to Christian commentaries on both the Old and the New. The New Testament, comprised of twenty-seven books authored not long after Jesus's life by more than a dozen men, is the fundamental basis of the Christian canon and most of early Christianity before disagreements over substance and administration divided it.

A part of that research was undertaken with an initially deep suspicion of accounts found within the classification of ancient scriptural books known as the apocryphal, meaning of doubtful authorship or authenticity, writings which are part of the Old Testament in Catholic and Byzantine Orthodox editions of Scripture but are not found in Jewish and Protestant editions. There is such a breadth of opinion about these writings Protestant label them outright as apocrypha while Catholics consider them deuterocanonical (second tier canonical). Differing timelines for in-or-out decision-making had much to do with the complex and long processes of determining their authenticity. The Jewish decision was made in the first century BC, and the Christian decision was near the end of the fourth century AD. Scholars regarded some texts as unquestionably unauthentic, but there were other reasons as to those which did not survive the initial authenticity tests. For example, an outright exclusion was one in which there was not known to be a Hebrew or Aramaic text prior to a known Greek text. Nineteenth- and twentieth-century archaeological discoveries of Hebrew texts were at least a millennium and a half in the future and would recast that conclusion for several questionable books from the first Christian century. With all of this in mind, I reduced but did not abandon my own skepticism of these texts, even finding some apocryphal accounts to be helpful in a fuller understanding of the history preceding and at the time of Jesus. My re-examination of biblical accounts and commentaries on them and my research into elements of what appears in these pages gave me a deeper understanding of Jesus, his relationships with his fishermen, and what they together accomplished on one hand and, in turn, what they expect of each of us.

Scriptural and other accounts of the Sea of Galilee, the livelihood of fishing on it, and life near it opened my research window into another dimension. They reached back thousands of years before and during the time of Jesus and his fishermen. They addressed the fishing techniques as well as the designs of boats and nets used and the species of fish caught and kept for compensation of crews, consumption by family and friends, commercial sales for the domestic market and preservation, and export to Rome and elsewhere. Throughout my writing, I recalled what I had experienced during my own travels along the Sea of Galilee and in Israel more widely, some of which experiences I shared in these pages.

The deeper I examined this account's facets, the more convinced I was that Jesus knew fishermen at the Sea of Galilee before the Gospels' accounts of him, walking its shoreline and asking his first disciples to follow him. I did not disbelieve the Gospels' accounts of the suddenness of his requests of them and their responses. Rather, I thought they expressed an historically dramatic conclusion without a fuller explanation preceding it, in short, the scriptural account is a conclusion without a setting out of its probable predicates. I believe Jesus already knew Peter and others before he called them with apparent abruptness to his ministry, his knowledge of them and theirs of him giving ready rise to their acceptance. He called two pairs of brothers, Simon and Andrew and James and John, a selection which achieved a certain tightness to his inner circle. Father Bargil Pixner, a Benedictine monk, archaeologist and author, made the point before his 2002 death that Jesus probably chose his disciples from among men from Galilee that he had seen in the company of John the Baptist at and near the time of his baptism. Is it a stretch to wonder if he discussed them and their attributes with John before he called them to his own ministry? Yes, but it is possible, if not probable, for they too had been baptized by and were among followers of John the Baptist, for we have no evidence that they were baptized after their call by Jesus.

John traveled in order to reach new communities of those wishing baptism. We know he baptized near Bethany, that geography being close to the communities of the Essenes, but you already know that from these pages.

The Galilean region was the location of much of Jesus's ministry of teaching and healing, and fishing for fish became far more than allegory for it became a model for persuading persons to follow his message. Words are words no matter from whom spoken, but his healing both affirmed his words and whom he said he was in his divine nature. His frustrations on one hand and the listeners' failures to comprehend on the other abated slowly, but miracles of healing sped that process, John describing his miracles as signs of that divinity. Jesus was complex, but so too was almost everything surrounding him and his followers, from Rome's oppressive occupation, through a deeply divided Judaism, to personal lives' certainties and uncertainties. After studying what others knew about Jesus living in Peter's mother-in-law's household in Capernaum, it became clearer to me that Jesus was more than casually aware of the principal occupation of that multi-generational family and that fishing is an occupation from which lessons, what we call best practices in our day, can be learned and explained in other contexts. I saw the need to include fishing into this text because it was such a central part of their lives and relationships.

As I struggled with that realization, I once abruptly stopped typing, looked down at my laptop keyboard, looked up at the text expanding on my screen and exclaimed aloud to the scarlet walls of the dining room in which I was writing, "My God, Jesus fished!" Yet, I did not know with certainty that he had fished with Peter and Peter's brother or any other disciple. I did know he could have accompanied them as they left their shared house to fish, especially if someone else needed for that task was unavailable for whatever reason. It is unfathomable to me that, as they left for their strenuous work, Jesus would not have sometimes offered to accompany them. Jesus was frequently abrupt with persons, including his disciples, but he was neither rude nor an ingratiate. "This is crazy," I thought, but I thought further of the matter. If he occasionally fished with his disciples, I wondered why we don't know about it, a possible answer being it was too obvious in those days of hardships as well as general knowledge of the occupation of fishing to consider setting it out in writings. Scripture informs us he was frequently along the shoreline in the company of his disciples and their boats, nets and even their netted fish. It was fish and bread that he multiplied. He used Peter's boat for transportation, even preaching from it as he moved out from crowds on shore, and crossing the lake to its eastern shore to test the willingness of a quite different audience to listen to his message. He even cooked a breakfast of fish and bread for them after their night of toiling on the water. I concluded that there needed to be discussions on the connections of Jesus, his Galilean fishermen, and the contexts of their lives as seen through the lens of two thousand years of scholarship by book and shovel. I felt their juxtapositions would tell us more than the Gospels highlighted.

The brevity of these pages could betray the volume of research which went into them. Its shorter length than many books is not a failure in producing a weightier, foot- or end-noted and door-stopping tome, for its intended value lay in the discussion of each of its focuses. My overarching priority was the telling of a fuller story of Jesus and his fishermen than Scripture alone tells us since that was not the Gospels' and acts of the apostolic authors' principal focus. Full truth be told, the research and writing evolved into a spiritual journey for me, and that came as a surprise. It was welcomed because it infused in me the mental and physical energies required to sustain the hours in the task.

There is more here than research, pondering and writing. It is an observation and a hope. The observation is that too few read texts about religion with an open mind. Is that a way of saying far too many read them with a closed mind? Not necessarily, but pre-disposition is both a defense of what is already known and often a rigid frame against additions to already held points of view. Yet, if a reader wants to read a lengthy compendium of differences on contexts, events, dates, locations, even names of places and persons and their spellings in original or English language translations, read the Bible for there are many seeming contradictions within its pages.

That awareness does not require a determination that if one is right all contrary to it must be wrong, such division arising from the Western canon in contrast to the Eastern faiths that conflicting truths can sit side by side without the necessity of harmonization, but in our way of thinking a defensive reaction often follows and immediately. To me, different recitations are similar to differences of perceived facts among a handful of witnesses to them, such as an automobile accident. There is no faster game of Gotcha! than accusing another of errors in their understandings of biblical texts. An open mind is helpful to learning and does not endanger a spiritual journey; as a matter of experience, it may strengthen it, even appreciably.

Does anything else need to be set out here? Yes, and they are in the nature of disclosures. I am not an academically trained scholar within any of the Abrahamic faiths of Judaism, Christianity, and Islam. I am a Christian, but I am not a priest or brother, minister or preacher, pastor, or other clergyman. I am a member of a congregation, most of its members, particularly myself, in greater need of living in accordance with the word in our lives than we admit to ourselves and to others. How many of us acknowledge that more is required for salvation than doing good works in those sectors of our communities singled out by Jesus in his reading at the Nazareth synagogue, his declaration in the Beatitudes and his directives to his apostles?

Responding affirmatively to those specific calls is of fundamental importance in appreciating what such responses demonstrate about the heart and mind of the giver of time, talent and treasure, but those actions are ancillary to the requirements of living in accordance with the Ten Commandments, reconciliation through repentance and redemption for not having done so, commitment not to repeat errors, and unilateral forgiveness of others for their transgressions against us, even without their forgiveness of us.

I am also not a PhD-credentialed historian although, like many who will read these pages, I take pride in knowing what I know, in holding my own when competitive facts are required in professional deliberations and social conversations. I do have three earned degrees, an honorary doctorate in law, and an honorary doctorate of humanities, and those focuses are relevant to these pages. When all of these qualifications are joined, I am still simply a layman but one who also fishes.

Not being a theologian or biblical scholar, how have I approached attitudinally the scriptural evidence necessary for these pages? It is a fair question, for scriptural accounts can seem inconsistent in our reading of them, sometimes in central and sometimes in peripheral ways. Issues posed for a writing based on scriptural accounts are inescapable. Confronted with each, I chose the scenario appearing to me as having the broadest consensus and to an extent differences of opinion remained important to the telling I set out the differing opinions.

A published history rests on contexts and facts known at the time it is reduced to a writing. To be complete in premises to assure the veracity of follow-on conclusions, a history must be updated in consideration of facts ascertained after its writing. Facts which come after a published writing update findings and conclusions relevant to it. It's a reason why new books appear on old subjects. To do otherwise would give that writing a shelf life after which it would become less accurate and therefore less relevant and less valuable as a research tool for others. A debilitating reality is that historians and others who adhere to a specific depiction in any field of study find it difficult to accept the consequences of new findings. This is especially true if their theses, dissertations, subsequent scholarship, and perhaps even income streams lock them immovably into conclusions challenged by the new findings. This is why an internationally respected laureate is said to have observed that progress in scholarship is made one funeral at a time. Historical analyses should be subject to that observation. They might or might not be in error, but whether one or the other should be a matter of very careful deliberation over time. In this, I am reminded of an observation made to me in respect to all faiths, that every doctrine was once a heresy; applied more broadly, every tradition began as an innovation, only his adjective "every" being suspect to me, for the observation is indeed generally true. His conclusion was not intended as a quip but rather to reflect a judgment of ninety years of his own scholarship in Jewish and Christian doctrines and traditions.

We need to underscore these points if we are to get the most out of what these pages posit. In mathematics, the truth of the sum requires accurate numbers. We have no accuracy if one or more numbers are not counted, subtracted, divided, or multiplied as the moment requires. In calculus, the locus depends on a correct reading of the intersection of sine and cosine. In logic, the accuracy of a conclusion rests on the inclusion of all considerations and their relative importance. To reflect further on the disciplines of historical analysis, the accuracy of a thesis rests upon inputs and their correlations, and new inputs and revised correlations never end. Each of these points, but especially those of history, are applicable to the Holy Land because archaeological and other discoveries and scholarship are reported initially, analyzed, and further reported. The discovery of nearly 1,000 scrolls found prior to 1947 in pottery jars in the Qumran caves near the shore of the Dead Sea made much international news, but they only added to similar earlier discoveries in the region of ancient writings. There were other similar findings too. The decades of tedious scholarship which followed as to their authenticity and content came slowly and with far less press and public attention. That had become the work of a scholarly few. That's why there are experts in such matters. We should neither cut off the flow of new information nor not work on how the new integrates with the existing. Reformulated conclusions are most often found in the spaces between denials and affirmations.

In the enormous digital research world classroom in which we now live, it is naïve to believe that the last word has been written on much of anything. When I was in secondary school, I was informed by a teacher of five steps in problem solving: (1) identification of a problem by the posing of a question, (2) statement of a hypothesis, (3) experimentation, (4) observation, and (5) drawing a tentative conclusion. Done many times in succession, it would move the researcher toward a more conclusive answer, weakening or affirming the tentative conclusion. It worked in that class as well as in others. I did not suspect at that time that it would apply to a broader range of studies at university, graduate schools, and life generally, but it did. Add to that method an attitude that two or more ought to be able to disagree without being disagreeable, I also experienced reduced barriers to new learning. Sharing points of view and on what bases they rest can have that effect.

In my opinion this methodology and that attitude ought to apply to each field of study associated with these pages: archaeology, astronomy, biography, biology, Christology, climatology, eschatology, genetics, geography, geology and paleogeology, geometry, heresiology, historiography, hydrology and hydrography, ichthyology, iconography, limnology, linguistics, literature, maritime history, mathematics, musicology, mythology, neurophysiology, oenology, orography, papyrology, phenomenology, philology, philosophy, phycology, psychology, sociology, symbology, theology, topography, volcanology, a few other disciplines, and the complexity of connecting them. The intersection of the method just described and these fields is central to deliberations focused on this region in the times in which Jesus lived and now.

Archaeological digs, which seem to be all around me when I travel in the region, followed by authentications of what knowledge came from them, are changing what we know and how the findings are integrated with other disciplines. A particular dig may be, and often is, controversial because of where it was or what it discovered, but such digs are essential to knowing more accurately the history of the region. A dig is sometimes controversial, even in advance of it, because of those opposing it believe it may disclose something contrary to the position held by those opponents. During the centuries of the Ottoman Empire's overlay of the Holy Land, archaeology within its provinces and vassal states was controlled primarily by the dual authorities of central political governance and the Patriarchates of the Eastern Orthodox Church. Well intended though those policies and practices may have been, they slowed but did not end authenticating research. In addition to digs by professionally competent archaeologists, there were also digs at which less competent professionals or unabashed looters destroyed sites and removed valuable artifacts whose study would have added to knowledge of region and religion. There were exceptions, and the discovery from 1898 into the early twentieth century at Oxyrhynchus (modern el-Bahnasa) in Egypt of an estimated half a million literary and other papyri manuscripts from the third century BC into the seventh century AD is particularly noteworthy, for they included a horde of ancient Hebrew and early Christian texts, some foreshadowing in appearance and content those found a half-century later near the Dead Sea. So too did those discovered in Egypt at Nag Hammadi. The realignment of national borders following the demise of the Ottoman Empire multiplied archaeological problem solving but created new opportunities. Archaeology is only one field in which valuable knowledge is now being rapidly expanded within the region.

There is little that people can do that is more informative to their understanding of the Scripture they have heard and read than to visit the Holy Land. A reading in which a referenced location is relevant is far more meaningfully understood if in its relation to another location and you have been to both. Where was the place from which Jesus asked for the donkey and foal on which he would ride into Jerusalem amidst celebratory palms and branches? How far away was it then and is now to the Lion's Gate or Sheep's Gate through which most believe he made his entry into the walled Jerusalem? How far was that gate in later exiting Jerusalem for Gethsemane at which he prayed so fervently? A mile or two? No, just a brief walk of several hundred yards or meters across the narrow

Kidron Valley. You are transformed in your thinking at each place of the Old and the New Testaments when next hearing another person reading aloud or you reading silently by having walked such steps, be they along the Sea of Galilee or in Bethlehem, Nazareth, Jerusalem or elsewhere. Be they along the Valley of Elah's stream bed from which David gathered five smooth stones to choose the one with which he would slay Goliath. Be they at the Copse of Trees at Endor in the Jazreel Valley at which a medium conjured the prophet Samuel to inform King Saul that he would die the next day. At nearby Mount Gilbao where Saul and his sons were killed by the Philistines. At Shiloh where the Ark of the Covenant was in tabernacle until moved, after having been lost in battle, to David's Jerusalem. And there are many sites in modern Israel's overlaying of that ancient Israel. They are all only one or a few plane flights from where you are reading these pages. By the way, take them with you and read specific pages. There is much to experience personally, including the historical events and places of the 2,000 years which separate the focus of this book from our lives.

At the beginning of the twenty-first chapter of John, Simon Peter said to those around him, "I go afishing," Πάω για ψάρεμα in Greek though he almost certainly said it in Aramaic. I have that quote framed in our residence's enclosed balcony, which houses fishing art work, photographs, trophies and other paraphernalia, together memories, together this exultation. It is mounted over a reproduction of an early depiction of Jesus's call to Peter and Andrew. It is a phrase said many millions of times and in many other contexts by fishers from millennia before Peter, through his life, to this day. It will continue to be exclaimed for as long as we and those that follow us are allowed to fish.

I hope you will agree with me that the words of these pages have given important contexts to the lives of Simon Peter, Andrew,

James, and John and, more important, to Jesus and to their real and allegorical ties to fish and fishing. Knowledge can be acquired, as I trust it has been here, to be stirred into that which was already known, the learner more informed as a consequence.

I conclude this book, but I will never conclude my search for additional facts and insights into their contexts, contents, and relationships, and I trust these pages have energized the reader's searches toward those facts and insights. A goal in these pages was to connect dots in ways that others may not have yet connected them. I will continue connecting old and new dots of what we know about Jesus's depictions of what we ought to be doing in our time, each of us, one by one, in my case to live the life he wished for me to live, for I am far short of that end goal, trusting that my repentance and belief in him as the son's nature of God are sufficient. That speaks to me, and it may speak also to you, for we are each and all left with what speaks to humanity.

A reader may be comfortably informed or baffled by these accounts, but the answer depends on the reader, and each is free to choose for himself.

If you are an atheist, you may reject all of this telling.

If you are agnostic, you may ponder it further, perhaps at length, not accepting some points while not rejecting others.

If you believe Jesus was a teacher of such note he became the centerpiece of Earth's largest religious denomination nearly 2,000 years later, you may rest comfortable with those thoughts.

If you regard Jesus as possibly divine, acknowledging circumstances in his life beyond our understanding but still believable upon more learning and deeper reflection, you may open wider the door to continued thought.

If you regard Jesus as divine, an incarnation on Earth from other than Earth, you have recognized his conception, birth, life, transfiguration, crucifixion, and resurrection, as well as the body of his teaching and the truth of his miracles which occurred with intended meaning for each of us and others.

Acknowledgment of Sources

While each reference below informed me across latitudinal and longitudinal scales of scholarship, I agreed with most, disagreed with others, and remained unsure about some, each a doorway to further inquiry by me and now by my readers. Each reader will reach their own conclusion about religion generally, faiths and their tied cultures, and about individual spiritual journeys. I am non-judgmental in respect to some references and even added others primarily for their provocative content. Here are all:

Acts of the Apostles; Myra Kahn Adams's "Miracles in the Hebrew Bible"; Sohrab Ahmari's *The Unbroken Thread: Discovering the Wisdom of Tradition in an Age of Chaos*; online Catholic news service Aleteia; American Bible Society; American Journal of International Law; the American–Israeli Cooperative Enterprises' Jewish Virtual Library; American School of Oriental Research; *Ancient History Encyclopedia*; Kate Andrews's "In pursuit of another epiphany"; Angel Studios' "The Chosen"; *Antiquaries Journal*; *Archaeological Encyclopedia of the Holy Land*; Kenneth Arnold's *Night Fishing in Galilee: The Journey Toward Spiritual Wisdom*; Amotz Asa-El's *Spectacular Israel* edited by Shai Ginott; Lamorna Ash's *Don't Forget We're Here Forever: A New Generation's Search for Religion*; Associated Press and its AP News; Associates for Biblical Research; Association for Jewish Studies; Association of Catholic Ordinaries of the Holy Land; Alan J. Avery-Peck and Jacob Neusner's *Judaism in Late Antiquity 4: Death, Life-After-Death, Resurrection, and the World-to-Come in the Ju-*

daisms of Antiquity; Michael Avi-Yonah's "The Walls of Nehemiah"; Michael Avi-Yonah and Emil G. Kraeling's *Our Living Bible.*

Barbara Ball, editor, *Understanding The Boat from the Time of Jesus*; Gary Ball-Kilbourne, editor, *Journey Through the Bible* series; Jordan Ballor and Eric J. Hutchinson's "Forgiveness as a Political Necessity"; Bishop Robert Barron's "Word on Fire"; John Barton's *A History of the Bible: The Book and Its Faiths*; Richard Bauckham's *Jesus and the Eyewitnesses: The Gospels as Eyewitness Testimony*; Mary Beard's *Twelve Caesars*; John A. Beck's *Everyday Life in Bible Times* and *The Holy Land for Christian Travelers*; Barry J. Beitzel's *The New Moody Atlas of the Bible*; Pope Benedict XVI's *Jesus of Nazareth*, Carol Ann Bernheim, Deepa Bharath's "New California museum offers immersive experience of Shroud of Turin," Bible texts from a King James' translation through modern translations; Bible History Daily; Bible Hub; BibleGateway; Bible League International; BiblePlaces.com; *Bible Odyssey*; BibleSEO.com; *Bible Study*; BibleStudyTools.com; BibleTeacher.org; *Biblical Archaeological Review*; Olivier Binst; Robert Polidori et al., *The Levant: History and Archaeology in the Eastern Mediterranean*; Harold Bloom's "Who Was Jesus and What Happened to Him?" in his *Jesus and Yahweh: The Names Divine*; Howard Blum's *The Gold of Exodus: The Discovery of the True Mount Sinai*; Todd Bolen's "Fishing on the Sea of Galilee"; Daniel Boyarin's "*Logos*: a Jewish Word: John's Prologue as Midrash"; Yeshuah Boyton; David Brakke's "Understanding the New Testament"; George Brantl, editor, *Christianity: Catholicism*; BreakingIsraelNews; Shannon Bream's *The Women of the Bible Speak*; *Britannica Encyclopedia of World Religions*; British Mandate for Palestine (formally Franco–British Convention on Certain Points Connected with the Mandates for Syria and the Lebanon, Palestine and Mesopotamia); Bill Broadway's "Digging Back Toward Jesus"; David Brooks's "My Decade-Long Journey to Belief"; E. Bruce Brooks's *Jesus and After: The First Eighty Years*; Kelly Brown's "The Art of Forgiveness"; Michael Brown's "God Uses Imperfect People"; Peter Brown's *Through the Eye of a Needle: Wealth, the Fall of Rome, and the Making of Christianity in the West, 350–550 AD* and *The Rise of Western Christendom: Triumph and Diversity, A.D. 200–1000*, and "The Other Rome," R.E. Brown. et al., *Peter in the New Testament*; Robert Browning's "A Death in the Desert";

James Bruce's "Reading the Hebrew Bible"; John M. Vonder Bruegge's *Mapping Galilee in Josephus, Luke, and John: Critical Geography and the Construction of Ancient Space*; Josephus' Galilee and Spatial Theory"; Anthony Brundage's *Going to the Sources: A Guide to Historical Research and Writing*; Rolin Bruno's *John and the Jesus Boat* series; Frederick Buechner's *The Remarkable Ordinary* and *A Crazy, Holy Grace*; Eugene Burnand's "God's Law of Love: A Spirituality of the Ten Commandments"; Tara Isabella Burton, David Vaaknin, and Jason Lee's "Divine Intervention."

Beit Galilee Yigal Allon Boat Museum: Orna Cohen (conservation process director 1986-2000), Niza Kaplan (museum manager), Rene Sivan (curator), Dorit Harel (Harel Designers), Hanan Hevron (architect), Uri Harmel (engineer) and their staffs as well as The Israel National Tourist Company and the Bracha Foundation.

Thomas Cahill's *Desire of the Everlasting Hills: The World Before and After Jesus*; Taylor Caldwell's *Dear and Glorious Physician*; Joseph Campbell's *The Masks of God* and other works in religion and mythology; Daniel Caner's *The Rich and the Pure: Philanthropy and the Making of Christian Society in Early Byzantium*; Nicholas Cannariato's "What is the afterlife?"; Dolores Cannon's *Jesus and the Essenes*; James Cannon's *Apostle Paul*: Cardinal Raniero Cantalamessa's homily at the Vatican's Good Friday 2022 liturgy; Maurice Casey's *Jesus of Nazareth: An Independent Historian's Account of His Life and Teaching*; *Catholic Encyclopedia*; Catholic News Agency's "Why Turn the Other Cheek?"; Centennial Media's *Jesus: The Light of the World*; Center for Israel Studies at Yeshiva University; Oswald Chamber's *Biblical Psychology: Christ-Centered Solutions for Daily Problems*; Georges Chevrot's *Simon Peter*; Christian Iconography; *Christian Post*; *Christian Research Journal*; Christianity.com; *Christianity Today*; Centennial Media; Owen Chadwick's *The Early Church* and *A History of Christianity*; Bruce Chilton's *The Herods: Murder, Politics, and the Art of Succession*; Wally V. Cirafesi's *Capernaum: Jews and Christians in the Ancient Village from the Time of Jesus to the Emergence of Islam*; Rodney Clapp's *A Peculiar People*; Arthur C. Clarke's "Profiles of the Future: An Inquiry into the Limits of the Possible"; Elesah Coffman's "What is the origin of the Christian fish symbol?"; Shaye J.D. Cohen's *Ancient Israel:*

From Abraham to the Roman Destruction of the Temple and "Judaism and Jewishness"; C.R. Condor's *The Bible and the East* and *Memoires: The Survey of Western and Eastern Palestine*; Kelly Corrigan's "If You Think You Cannot Forgive, Remember, You Do It All the Time"; F.L. Cross, editor, *The Oxford Dictionary of the Christian Church*; Andrew Crumey's "Finding God in the Details"; John D. Currid and David P. Barrett's *ESV Bible Atlas*; Michael B. Curry's "Word to the Church: Who shall we be?"

Gustaf Dalman's *Jesus-Jeshua: Studies in the Gospels, Sacred Sites and Ways: Studies in the Topography of the Gospels* and *Work, and Customs in Palestine*; John Daniel Davidson's "Teach Your Children Well"; Chuck Davis's *Authority Encounters: Embracing God's Mission for You*; Dead Sea Scrolls Foundation; *Delitzsch's Hebrew New Testament*; David DeSteno's "Is Religion Good for Your Health?"; Donald J. Devine's "The Civilizational Choice" in *The Enduring Tension*; Amanda DeWitt's "Passing the Hope of Jesus to the Next Generation"; Anna Dintaman and David Landis's *Walking the Jesus Trail: Nazareth to the Sea of Galilee*; Discipleship Ministries; Jean Doresse's *The Discovery of the Nag Hammadi Texts*; Ross Douthat's "How to Think Your Way Into Religious Belief," "The Benefits of a Naïve Reading of the Gospels," "God and Miracles: A Conversation," and *Believe: Why Everyone Should Be Religious*; Rod Dreher's *Live Not By Lies* and *The Benedict Option*; Owen Francis Dudley's *Will Men Be Like Gods?*; J. Leslie Dunstan, editor, *Christianity: Protestantism.*

Ecole Biblique; Timothy Egan's *A Pilgrimage to Eternity*; EarlyChristianWritings.com; Egeria's *Diary of a Pilgrimage* in various translations; Barbara Ehrenreich's *Living with a Wild God*; Robert Eisler's *Jesus's Sermon to the Galilean Fishermen* and *Fish Symbolism in the Early Christian Literature*; T.S. Eliot's "Notes Toward the Definition of Culture"; Walter A. Elwell, editor, *Encyclopaedia Britannica*; *Encyclopedia Judaica*, *Encyclopaedia of the Bible*; *Encyclopedia of Christian Theology*; *Encyclopedia of the Dead Sea Scrolls*; Joe R. Engel and David Brakke's *Understanding the New Testament*; David D. Ehrman's *How Jesus Became God*; Eusebius of Caesarea's *The History of the Church from Christ to Constantine* in translations; David Ewert's *A General Introduction to the Bible: From Ancient Tablets to Modern Translations.*

Michael Fagenblat's "The Concept of Neighbor in Jewish and Christian Ethics"; Mary Fairchild's "20 Famous Women of the Bible"; FaithMedia, Carol Andrews, editor, and Raymond O. Faulkner, translator, *The Ancient Egyptian Book of the Dead*; A. R. Fausset's *Bible Dictionary*; Fellowship of Israel Related Ministries (FIRM); Everett Ferguson's "When did the cross supplant the ichthus (fish) as a symbol of Christianity?"; Ferrell's Travel Blog; Edward Feser's *Immortal Souls* and "A robust philosophical defense of the immortality of the soul"; Leslie Leyland Field's *Crossing the Waters*; David A. Fiensy and James Riley Strange's *Galilee in the Late Second Temple and Mishnaic Periods*; Steven Fine's "Art and Judaism in the Greco-Roman World: Toward a New Jewish Archaeology"; Jack Finegan's *Handbook of Biblical Chronology*; Israel Finkelstein and Neil Asher Silberman's *The Bible Unearthed*; Fishers of Men Ministries; David Flusser's *Judaism and the Origins of Christianity*; Charlotte Elisheva Fonrobert's "Judaizers, Jewish Christians and Others"; H.H. Francis's *Fratelli Tutti (Brothers All)*; Franciscan Foundation for the Holy Land; Paula Fredriksen's *Augustine and the Jews: A Christian Defense of Jews and Judaism* and *When Christians Were Jews: The First Generation*; Neal B. Freeman's *Walk with Me: An Invitation to Faith*; David M. Freidenreich's "Food and Table Fellowship"; Sean Freyne's *Galilee from Alexander the Great to Hadrian, 323 B.C.E. to 135 C.E.* and "The Geography, Politics and Economics of Galilee."

Galilee boat project team: Shelley Wachsmann (co-director and as referenced below), Kurt Raveh (co-director of excavation and maritime archaeologist), Orna Cohen (conservator), Moshe and Yuval Lufan (discoverers of the boat and logistics), J. Richard Steffy (ship reconstructor and noted below), Danny Friedman, C. Amit and Dubi Gal (photographers), Edna Amos (registrar and final plans drawings), and members of Kibbutz Ginosar who assisted throughout.

Richard A. Gard, editor, *Great Religions of Modern Man*; Robert Garland's *The Other Side of History: Daily Life in the Ancient World*; John H. Garvey's *The Virtues*; Andrea Garza-Díaz's "The Archaeological Excavations at Magdala"; Gefen Publishing House Ltd. and its Gefen Books and Ora Cummings; Woodrow A. Geier's *John*; R. Douglas Geivett's *Evil and the Evidence for God* and *Contemporary Perspectives on Religious Epistemology*; Georgetown University's Center for Jewish Civilization and Berkley Center for Religion, Peace and World Affairs; German Association of the Holy Land (originally named German Palestine Association); German Catholic Society for Palestine; German Oriental Society; Mark Gerson's "Passover and the Power of Jewish Continuity"; Michael Gerson's "The defiant hope of Christmas: God is with us"; Etienne Gilson's *Reason and Revelation in the Middle Ages*; Jack Gist's "Learning Virtue in the Postmodern Wilds"; GluedIdeas.com; Patrick Glynn's *God: The Evidence—The Reconciliation of Faith and Reason in a Postsecular World*; Norman Golb's *Who Wrote the Dead Sea Scrolls?*; David P. Goldman's "Reason to Believe"; Justo Gonzalez's *The Story of Christianity*; Philip Goodchild's "Jesus Boat"; Martin Goodman's *Herod The Great: Jewish King in a Roman World* and "Jewish History, 331 BC–135 CE"; Micah Goodman's *The Wondering Jew: Israel and the Search for Jewish Identity*; Gospel-Mysteries.net; Martin Goodman's *A History of Judaism* and *Rome and Jerusalem: A Clash of Ancient Civilizations*; Ernest Gordon's "Faith and Thought" in his *Me, Myself and Who?*; Gospel of Mary Magdalene; Gospels of Matthew, Mark, Luke and John, and *The Acts of the Apostles* and commentaries thereon; Gospel of Thomas; GotQuestions.org; gracetogospel.com, Michael Grant's *Saint Peter: A Biography* and *The Jews in the Roman World*; Jim Graves's "Shroud Shows What Jesus Endured for Our Salvation"; Arthur Green's *Judaism for the World: Reflections on God, Life and Love*; Dominic Green's "Rome's Man in Jerusalem" and "A Faith Finds Its Feet"; Billy Graham's *Where I Am: Heaven, Eternity, and Our Life Beyond the Now*, B. P. Grenfell and A. S. Hunt's "The Oxyrhynchus papyri" series and *Sayings of Our Lord from an Early Greek Papyrus*; Romano Guardini's *The Lord*; Rafael D. Guererro III's "St. Peter's Fish in Israel"; Mary I. Guyton, et al., *Judea Trembles Under Rome.*

Haaretz; Rudolf de Haas's "Galilee, the Sacred Sea"; Christopher A. Hall's *Reading Scripture with the Church Fathers*; Billy Hallowell's "Youth movement driving America's return to the Bible," Graham Hancock's *The Sign and the Seal*; Harvard University's Center for Jewish Studies; K.C. Hanson and Douglas Oakman's *Palestine in the Time of Jesus*; David Bentley Hart's *The Experience of God*; Fredric Hasselquist's *Voyages and Travels in the Levant*; James Hastings, et al., *A Dictionary of Christ and the Gospels*; C. Michel Hawn's "History of Hymns: 'Deep River'"; David Hazony's *The Ten Commandments: How Our Most Ancient Moral Text Can Revive Modern Life*; Peter Heather's *Christendom: The Triumph of a Religion, AD 300–1300*; Alfred J. Hebert's *Raised from the Dead: True Stories of 400 Resurrection Miracles*; Hebrew University of Jerusalem and its Institute of Archeology; Niels Hemmingsen's (as edited and translated by Eric J. Hutchinson) *On the Law of Nature*; Steve Hendrix and Sarah Dadouch's "Israel shells Lebanon after a rocket attack in Galilee"; Paul Herrick's *Philosophy, Reasoned Belief, and Faith*; Arthur Hertzberg, editor, *Judaism*; Abraham Joshua Heschel's *The Sabbath*; Michael Hesemann's *Jesus of Nazareth: Archaeologists Retracing the Footsteps of Christ*; Martha Himmelfarb's "Afterlife and Resurrection," Historic Mysteries; Eugene Hoade's *Guide to the Holy Land*; Harold W. Hoehner's *Chronological Aspects of the Life of Christ*; Tom Holland's *Dominion: How the Christian Revolution Remade the World*; Lauren Holtzblatt's "In Judaism, Our Words Matter"; James Hornell's *Fishing in Many Waters* and *Report of the Fisheries of Palestine*; Richard A. Horsley's *Archaeology, History and Society in Galilee: The Social Context of Jesus and the Rabbis*; House of Anchors Fishing Museum at Kibbutz Ein Gev; Victor Hulbert's "Walking with Jesus in Galilee"; Samuel P. Huntington's "The Clash of Civilizations?"; Robert J. Hutchinson's *The Dawn of Christianity*.

Lauren Ibach's *The Bible in a Year*; International Fellowship of Christians and Jews; International Forgiveness Institute; International Jewish Committee on Interreligious Consultations; *International Journal of Nautical Archaeology*; *International Standard Bible Encyclopedia*; Jean-Pierre Isbouts's *Archaeology and the Bible: The Greatest Discoveries from Genesis to the Roman Era, From Moses to Muhammad: The Shared Origins of Judaism, Christianity and Islam, Young Jesus: Restoring the "Lost Years" of a Social Activist and Religious Dissidents, Jesus: An Illustrated Life, The Story of Christianity: A Chronicle of Christian Civilization from Ancient Rome to Today, In the Footsteps of Jesus: A Chronicle of His Life and the Origins of Christianity* revised and republished as *Jesus and the Origins of Christianity, Atlas of the Bible: Exploring the Holy Lands*, and *The Dead Sea Scrolls: 75 Years Since Their Historic Discovery* (National Geographic), IsraelByFoot.

com; Israel Exploration Society; Fred Israel's "Profiles in Spirituality: Fred Israel on Jews, Jesuits, and Natura Laws" and his wife Lesley and their Herman Allen Israel Endowed Lectureship in Jewish–Catholic Relations at Georgetown University; Israel Institute of Biblical Studies; Israel Ministry of Education and its Antiquities Authority; Israel Ministry of Foreign Affairs; Israel Ministry of Jerusalem Affairs and Heritage; Israel Ministry of Tourism generally and the Gospel Trail particularly; Israel Ministry of Water and Agriculture, its Fishing and Agriculture Division, and its National Water Carrier (Medkorot); Israel Oceanographic and Limnological Research Ltd., ISRAEL21c (an American online magazine).

Gregory Jantz's "The Secret Weapon for Mental Health: Forgiveness"; Owen Jarus's "Mysterious Stone Structure Discovered Beneath Sea of Galilee"; Ken Jennings's *100 Places to See After You Die*; Jerusalem Perspective; *Jerusalem Post*; Jesus Seminar published papers; The Jesus Trail Team and its JesusTrail.com; JesusWalk.com; Jewish Theological Seminary; Jewish Virtual Library; *The Jewish Week*; H.H. John Paul II's *Papal Encyclicals of John Paul II (1978–2005)*; Paul Johnson's *A History of Christianity, A History of the Jews*, and *Jesus: A Biography from a Believer*; Jordan Department of Antiquities; Jordan Tourism Board; Titus Flavius Josephus's *The Jewish War* and *Antiquities of the Jews* in multiple translations of title and text.

Eric Kampmann and colleagues' "The Everyday Bible Study," Timothy Keller's *The Reason for God: Belief in an Age of Skepticism* also published as *The Reason for God, Making Sense of God*, and "What Too Little Forgiveness Does to Us"; Tim Keesee's "Worshipping God at the Ends of the Earth"; Thomas á Kempis's *The Imitation of Christ*; Titus M. Kennedy's *Unearthing the Bible: 101 Discoveries That Bring the Bible to Life*; William R. Kenan, Jr.'s *The Myth of Christian Beginnings*; R.T. Kendall and David Rosen's *The Christian and the Pharisee: Two Outspoken Religious Leaders Debate the Road to Heaven*; Malcolm H. Kerr's *The Arab Cold War* (2020 edition), Isabel Kershner's "In Israel, Ominous Lessons from Ancient Past"; Kibbutz Ein Gev and its Tourist Department; Kibbutz Ginosar and its leadership and members; Karen L. King's *The Gospel of Mary Magdala*; Patrick Kingsley's "Digging Into Their Town's Past, Right

Below Their Homes"; Paul Kingsnorth's *Savage Gods*; Kinneret Academic College and its Kinneret Institute for Galilean Archaeology; Kinneret Sailing Co.; Linda Kinstler's "Can Silicon Valley Find God?"; Jonathan Klawans's "The Law"; David Whitmarsh Knight's *William Blake's "Jerusalem" Explained*; Knowing-Jesus.com; Nikos Kokkinos's *The Herodian Dynasty*; Moshe Koppel's *Judaism Straight Up: Why Real Religion Endures*; Ross S. Kraemer's "Jewish Family Life in the First Century CE"; Jamie Kreiner's *The Wandering Mind*; James Kwak's "Why the wheels of human history seemed to turn faster for some."

Lamb and Lion Ministries; D. Thomas Lancaster's *Restoration: Returning the Torah of Moses to the Disciples of Jesus*, *Elementary Principles: Six Foundational Principles of Ancient Jewish Christianity*, and *Grafted In: Israel, Gentiles, and the Mystery of the Gospel*; Andrew Lawler's *Under Jerusalem*; Harper Lee's "Christmas to Me" now in her HarperCollins Publishers' *The Land of Sweet Forever*; Learn Religions; John Legend's "Roll Jordan Roll"; Vincent Lemire et al., *Jerusalem: History of a Global City*; Leo XIV's build the Church on the solid foundations of Christ, not on worldly criteria, Rebecca Lesses's "Divine Beings"; David B. Levenson's "Messianic Movements"; Outi Lehtipuu's *Debates Over the Resurrection of the Dead*; Jon D. Levenson's *Resurrection and the Restoration of Israel*; Beatrice Levertoff's "The Death of Paul Levertoff"; Paul P. Levertoff's *Love and the Messianic Age*; Amy-Jill Levine and Mark Zvi Brettler's, editors, *The Jewish Annotated New Testament* New Revised Standard Version; C.S. Lewis's *Mere Christianity* and "Is All Love Created Equal?"' Libolt Brunton and Graber's *Redeeming the West: A Christian Defense of Reason and Individualism, LIFE*'s *Women of the Bible*; LiveScience; Richard Longenecker, editor, *Life in the Face of Death: The Resurrection Message of the New Testament*; Max Lucado's *Jesus: The God Who Knows Your Name*; T.M. Luhrmann's *How God Becomes Real*.

John D. and Catherine T. MacArthur Foundation; Diarmaid MacCulloch's *Christianity: The First Three Thousand Years* and "The Vitality of Orthodoxy"; Neil MacGregor with Erika Langmuir's *Seeing Salvation: Images of Christ in Art*; Esau McCaulley's "Why I Am Still a Christian"; Tim and Lydia McGrew's "How the Gospels Pass the Historical Test";

Rebecca McLaughlin's *Confronting Christianity: Twelve Hard Questions for the World's Largest Religion* and "When Mary Met the Angel"; Jodi Magness's *The Holy Land Revealed*; David Marchese's "Jonathan Roumie Plays Jesus to Millions"; Nur Masalha's *Palestine: A Four Thousand Year History*; Steve Mason's *A History of the Jewish War: A.D. 66–74*; Jules Massenet's *Hérodiade*; Ernest W. Gurney Masterman's *Studies in Galilee*; William Steuart McBirnie's *The Search for the Twelve Apostles*; Esau McCaulley "The Unsettling Power of Easter," John Anthony McCuckin's *The Eastern Orthodox Church: A New History*; James McKeehan's *An Overview of the Old Testament and How It Relates to the New Testament*; Michael McKenna's "God or Madman: There Is No Third Option: The Story of an Obscure Jewish Carpenter"; John P. Meier's *A Marginal Jew: Rethinking the Historical Jesus*; Auguste Meyrat's "The Mundane, Not Just Miracles, Converts the World"; Sandra Miesels's "The often silent and surprising history of devotion to Saint Joseph"; Maria Rosa Menocal's *The Ornament of the World: How Muslims, Jews, and Christians Created a Culture of Tolerance in Medieval Spain*; Selah Merrill's *Galilee in the Time of Christ*; Thomas Merton's *The Seven Storey Mountain*; Bruce Manning Metzger's *The Oxford Companion to the Bible* and *The Oxford Guide to People & Places of the Bible*; Anne and Daniel Meurois-Givaudan's *The Way of the Essenes*; Stephen C. Meyer's *Return of the God Hypothesis*; James A. Michener's *The Source*; Sandra Miesel's "The often silent and surprising history of devotion to Saint Joseph"; Margaret Ruth Miles' *The Word Made Flesh: A History of Christian Thought*; J. Maxwell Miller and John H. Hayes' *A History of Ancient Israel and Judah*; Paul D. Miller's "Finding God at the End of History"; Troy A. Miller's "Christians are under attack"; Jeff Minick's "Turning Your Burdens into Blessings"; Martha Minow's *When Should Law Forgive?*; Samuel H. Moffett's *A History of Christianity in Asia: Beginnings to 1500*; Simon Sebag Montefiore's *Jerusalem: The Biography*; Raymond A. Moody's *Life After Life* and his and Paul Perry's *The Light Beyond*; Mother Teresa of Calcutta's *A Gift for God*; G. Fr. Ronald Murphy, SJ's "The Night Before He Suffered"; Jerome Murphy-O'Connor's *Oxford Archaeological Guides: The Holy Land*, Charles Murray's *Taking Religion Seriously* and "I now believe in God. My peers are in disbelief."

Mark D. Nanos's "Paul and Judaism," National Geographic Society's *Jesus and the Origins of Christianity*; *Atlas of the Bible: Exploring the Holy Lands, The Dead Sea Scrolls: 75 Years Since Their Historic Discovery* and their maps; Council of Centers on Jewish–Christian Relations, "A National Reckoning of the Soul: A Call to the Churches of the United States to Confront the Crisis of Antisemitism"; Nautical Archaeology Society and its Dr. Kurt Raveh; Yaacov Kahanov and Chris Brandon, *The New York Times*; Avraham Negev and Shimon Gibson's *Archaeological Encyclopedia of the Holy Land*; NewAdvent.org; George W.E. Nickelsburg's *Resurrection, Immortality, and Eternal Life*; Wallace Nichols' *Blue Mind*; Sam Nicholson's "A robust philosophical defense of the immortality of the soul"; R. Steven Notley, author of the foreword to *Understanding the Boat from the Time of Jesus*; Mendel Nun's *Ancient Jewish Fisheries* (Hebrew) sometimes referred to as *Ancient Jewish Fishing, The Sea of Galilee and Its Fisherman in the New Testament*, "A Life on the Kinneret: Fish, Storms and a Boat," "The Kingdom of Heaven Is Like a Seine," and "Let Down Your Nets"; Cardinal Nguyen Van Thuan's *Five Loaves and Two Fish.*

D.E. Oakman's *Jesus and the Economic Questions of His Day*; Peter Occhiogrosso's *The Joy of Sects*; Gerald O'Collins's *Jesus: A Portrait*; Odetta's "Deep River"; George Ogg's *The Chronology of the Public Ministry of Jesus*; Daniel Oliver's "The Good Samaritan, William Blake, and the Wicked State"; Carl E. Olson's *Did Jesus Really Rise from the Dead?*, "Sinners, Apostles, Martyrs: On the Solemnity of Saints Peter and Paul," and "We are called to fishers of men"; *The Oxford Encyclopedia of Archaeology*; *The Oxford Illustrated History of Christianity* edited by John McManners; the Oxford University Oxyrhynchus Papyri project.

Elaine Pagels's *Beyond Belief: The Secret Gospel of Thomas,*; *The Gnostic Gospels* and *The Johannine Gospel in Gnostic Exegesis*; *The Historical Mystery of Jesus*; Palphot Ltd.'s "Pilgrims Map of The Holy Land" and its "Jesus's Journeys in The Holy Land," both drawn by Evgeny Barashkov; Blair Parke's "Ichthys, The Christian Faith Fish Symbol"; Tara Parker-Pope's "You can learn to forgive. Here's why you should"; Patheos; PBS's "Fiddler: Miracles of Miracles"; Nicholas Perrin's "Thomas: The Fifth Gospel?"; Tomer Persico's *In God's Image*, Francis E. Peters's *The*

Monotheists: Jews, Christians and Muslims in Conflict and Competition; James W. Peterson's *The Philosophy of Explanation*; Rogan, Joe. *"#1769—Jordan Peterson."* Podcast episode of *The Joe Rogan Experience*, January 25 2022. *Maps of Meaning: The Architecture of Belief, 12 Rules for Life: An Antidote to Chaos*, and *Beyond Order: 12 More Rules for Life*; Chandra Philip's "Acts of Kindness Ease Loneliness and Improve Mental Health," Ambassador Thomas R. Pickering and the staff of the U.S. Embassy in Israel and the U.S. Information Agency staff; David Pileggi's "A Life on the Kinneret"; Everett Piper's "Mistakes or sin? There's a big difference"; Brant Pitre's *Jesus and the Jewish Roots of the Eucharist*; Fr. Bargil Pixner, OSB's *With Jesus in Jerusalem His First and Last Days in Judea* and *With Jesus through Galilee According to the Fifth Gospel*; the Poetry Foundation; Jerry J. Pokorsky's "The Commandments and the restoration of civilization"; Reynolds Price's *Three Gospels.*

Abraham Rabinovich's "Sea of Galilee site's founding provides a look back in time: Archaeologists uncover Bethsaida, home to several apostles" and "'Jesus Boat' Causes Ripples"; Simcha Raphael's *Jewish Views of the Afterlife*; Joseph Ratzinger's (Pope Benedict XVI) *Jesus of Nazareth* and "The Truth of the Resurrection"; Kurt Raveh, director of Dor Archaeological Museum and the University of Haifa's Center for Maritime & Regional Archaeology and his "The Emotional Cargo of an Ancient Boat"; Norman S. Ream's *Reflections on Man and Nature*, ReasonsForHopeJesus.com; Annette Yoshiko Reed's *Jewish Christianity and the History of Judaism*; Lawrence W. Reed's *Was Jesus a Socialist?*; Aaron Renn's "The Evaporation of the Sacred" and "Fossilized Faith," Alfred S. Regnery's *Unlikely Pilgrim: A Journey into History and Faith*; David Reich's *Who We Are and How We Got Here: Ancient DNA and the New Science of the Human Past*; Religion News Service, Gary A. Rendsburg's *How the Bible Is Written*; Aaron Renn's "The Three Worlds of Evangelicalism," "The Blowback Against the Three World's Model," and *Life in the Negative World: Confronting Challenges in an Anti-Christian Culture*; Kevin Revolinski's "Dead Sea in Israel"; Daniel E. Ritchie's "A Hymn to Christ's Sacrifice"; James M. Robinson's *The Nag Hammadi Library in English*; Marilynne Robinson's *Reading Genesis*; Andrew Roberts' "Ancient Rome's Longest Rebellion"; Francis X. Rocca's "What Should Jesus Look Like?"; Kristin

Romey and Simon Norfolk's "The Search for the Real Jesus"; Mark Rooker's *The Ten Commandments: Ethics for the Twenty-First Century*; James Romm's "What Happened at Masasa?"; *Rose Book of Bible Charts, Maps and Time Lines*; the writings of the American Jewish Committee's International Director of Interreligious Affairs Rabbi David S. Rosen; Lily Rothman's "Lessons from Their Lives" in *Women of the Bible*; Robert M. Royalty's *The Origin of Heresy: A History of Discourse in Second Temple Judaism and Early Christianity.*

Jonathan Sacks's *Morality: Restoring the Common Good in Divided Times*; Sean Salai's "Importance of religion in daily lives hits new low for Americans," Salesian Missions of Don Bosco; Lauren Sarner's "Beyond Beliefs"; Leonard Sax's "Do You Have to Be Stupid to Believe in God?"; Fr. James V. Schall, SJ's "What Is 'The Nativity'?"; Sacred Destinations; E. P. Sanders's *The Historical Figure of Jesus*; Shlomo Sand's *The Invention of the Jewish People*; James V. Schall's "The Two Gods"; Lawrence H. Schiffman's *The Halakhah at Qumran* and *Who Was a Jew? Rabbinical Perspectives on the Jewish–Christian Schism*; Richard Schiffman's "Lessons on forgiveness move out of religious spaces and into schools"; Basilea Schlink's *The Holy Land Today*; Konrad Schmid and Jens Schroter's *The Making of the Bible from the First Fragments to Sacred Scripture*; Messianic Rabbi K.A. Schneider's "The Jewish Jesus," Fr. George E. Schultze, SJ's "Of All Things Visible and Invisible: Postmodernism and Unbelief"; Jennifer Schuessler's "A Fake? Or Biblical Gold?"; Emil Schurer's *A History of the Jewish People in the Time of Jesus Christ*; Daniel R. Schwartz's "Jewish Movements of the New Testament Period"; Albert Schweitzer's *The Quest of the Historical Jesus*; Roger Scruton's *The Face of God* and *The Soul of the World*; Sea of Galilee Administration, now known as the Sea of Galilee Authority; Paul Senz's "Archaeology and the historical truth of the Gospels"; Hershel Shanks's *Ancient Israel: From Abraham to the Roman Destruction of the Temple (3rd Edition)*, *Freeing the Dead Sea Scrolls*, *Jerusalem: An Archaeological Biography*, and, for the archaeological magazines which he published, Jane Shaw's "A mosaic of belief"; Bishop Fulton J. Sheen's *Life of Christ*; Yonat Shimron's "A documentary explores the ancient and modern practice of the Sabbath"; Yaakov Shkolnik; Ari Shavit's *My Promised Land*; Si Sheppard's *The Jewish Revolt, AD 66–74*; Joseph Sievers and

Amy-Jill Levine, editors, *The Pharisees,* including their "What We Don't Know Can Hurt Us: The Need and The Project" seminar; Ana Siljak's "The Idea That hanged Humanity," Skynews's "Race to Save Sea of Galilee from Disaster" report; Ninian Smart's *The Phenomenon of Christianity*; Christian Smith's *Why Religion Went Obsolete: The Demise of Traditional Faith in America*; George Adam Smith's *Historical Geography of the Holy Land*; Huston Smith's *The World's Religions*; (London's) Society for Promoting Christian Knowledge; the Society for Protection of Nature in Israel; Society of St. John the Evangelist, Oren Sonin's "Fisheries in the Roman Period and Fisheries in Israel Today"; Elizabeth Svoboda's "The Neuroscience of Morality," Willard Spiegelman's "Crucifixion: Reclaiming a Calamity"; Robert St. John's *Roll* Jor*dan Roll: The Life Story of a River and Its People*; Rodney Stark's *The Rise of Christianity: A Sociologist Reconsiders History*; J. Richard Steffy's *Wooden Ship Building andk the Interpretation of Shipwrecks*; Sarah Abrevaya Stein's *Family Papers: A Sephardic Journey Through the Twentieth Century*; Wayne Stiles's *Walking in the Footsteps of Jesus: A Journey Through the Lands and Lessons of Christ* and his "Walking the Bible Lands" series; Howard Storm's *My Descent into Death, Befriend God: Life with Jesus, Lessons Learned: A Spiritual Journey*, and *It's All Love*; Barry Strauss's *Jews vs. Rome*; Peter M.J. Stravinskas's "God's Law of Love: A Spirituality of the Ten Commandments" and "Who Is My Neighbor? On the Parable of the Good Samaritan." and Barton Swaim's "Faith Makes a Comeback."

Tailor Made Tours, Ltd.; Joan E. Taylor's *The Immerser: John the Baptist within Second Temple Judaism*; Titus Techera's "Modern Martyrdom"; Matthew Teller's *Nine Quarters of Jerusalem: A New Biography of the Old City*; William Temple's *Readings in St. John's Gospel*; Texas A&M University, its Institute of Nautical Archaeology, its D. Johnson, and its Ship Reconstruction Laboratory; The Bible and Interpretation; *The Expository Files,* The Fishing Museum Online; The Friends of Israel Outreach Ministry's *Israel My Glory*; *The Jerusalem Post*; *The Jewish Quarterly*; *The New York Times's Times of Israel*; *1,000 Places to See Before You Die*; *The Talbot Spy*; Theofilus III, patriarch of Jerusalem; Carston Peter Thiede's *Simon Peter: From Galilee to Rome*; *Time*; TimeAndDate.com, *Times Atlas of the Bible*; Krista Tippett's "Why Is It So Hard to Talk About God?";

Andrew Todhunter and Lynn Johnson's "The Apostles' Eternal Journey"; Leo Tolstoy's *On Life: A Critical Edition*, ed. by Inessa Medzhibovskaya and trans. from Russian by Michael Denner and Inessa Medzhibovskaya; Guido Tonelli's *Genesis, Touchstone: A Journal of Mere Christianity*; TripAdvisor.com, Reverend Henry Baker Tristram's *The Flora and Fauna of the Holy Land*; Fr. Zbigniew Tyburski's *The Encyclicals of John Paul II: Foundations of Catholic Faith and Morality*; Vassilios Tzaferis's *The Holy Land.*

UNESCO World Heritage Sites; Leon Uris's novel *Exodus*; the University of Bethlehem; the University of the Holy Land.

Carl Van Treeck and Aloysius Croft's *Symbols in the Church*; The Vatican and its Apostolic Delegation in Jerusalem; Geza Vermes's "Jewish Miracle Workers in the Late Second Temple Period"; *Vermont Catholic*'s "Still Fishers of Men"; Society of St. John the Evangelist's Br. David Vryhof's "Resurrection Narratives in the Fourth Gospel."

Shelley Wachsmann's *Seagoing Ships and Seamanship in the Bronze Age Levant, The Sea of Galilee Boat: The 2000 Year Old Discovery from the Sea of Legends*, and *Understanding The Boat from the Times of Jesus* (edited by Barbara Ball at CARTA Jerusalem and introduced by R. Steven Notley's foreword); James Walkin's *Amazing Grace: A Cultural History of the Beloved Hymn*; Matthew Walther's "The 'Messiah' Belongs to Everyone"; Menachem Weckler's "Acts of Faith"; Peter Wehner's "Why Jesus Loved Friendship"; George Weigel's "The Easter Effect," "From Christendom Times to Apostolic Times," *To Sanctify the World*, "The grave sin of Jew-hatred," "Following the Jewish Jesus," "Antisemitism is a betrayal of Christianity, for Jew-hatred is Christ-hatred," and *Pomp, Circumstance, and Unsolicited Advice*; Barri Weiss's "You Are the Last Line of Defense"; Stephen Weizman's "Ancient Galilee church unearthed, said to be home to apostles Peter and Andrew"; Morris West's novel *The Shoes of the Fisherman*; Bruce Wetterau's *World History*; J.S. Whale's *Christian Doctrine*; Wikimedia and Wikimedia Commons; Wikipedia texts available under the Creative Commons Attribution–ShareAlike license; Wikipedia Foundation, Inc., and Wikipedia Commons; John Alden Williams, editor, *Islam*; Mary Robb D. Wilson's *Soul Shine*; Ralph F. Wilson's "Early Christian Symbols in the Catacombs"; Christian Wiman's *My Bright Abyss*; Lea Lofenfeld Winkler and Ramit Frenkel's *The Boat and the Sea of Galilee*; Matthew Wiseman's *The Two Jerusalems*; *World Archaeology*; World History Encyclopedia; Molly Worthen's "How Would You Prove That God Performed a Miracle?"; Everett Worthington's *Forgiving and Reconciling: Bridges to Wellness and Hope* and *Moving Forward: Six Steps to Forgiving Yourself and Breaking Free from the Past*; N.T. Wright's *Luke for Everyone* and *Paul and the Faithfulness of God*; N.T. Wright and Michael F. Bird's *Jesus and the Powers: Christian Political Witness in an Age of Totalitarian Terror and Dysfunctional Democracies*; Donald W. Wuerl, Ronald Lawler, and Thomas Comerford Lawler, editors, *The Teaching of Christ*; Stephen M. Wylen's *The Jews in the Time of Jesus: An Introduction.*

David B. Yaden and Andrew B. Newberg's *The Varieties of Spiritual Experience: 21st Century Research and Perspectives*; Sarah Young's *Jesus Calling* and *Jesus Listens*; Terry Young's *After the Fishermen.*

Xulon Press.

David Zahl's *Low Anthropology: The Unlikely Key to a Gracious View of Others (and Yourself)*; Karlos Zurutuza's "Disciples of St. John the Baptist under attack."

While this book is not a children's book, I noted in my research that Margaret Ayer, Barbara Fleming, Emil Maier, Mirriam Mosha, Marc Olson and Jim Maybank, Vic Parker, Sophie Piper and Estelle Corke, Mary Richardson, and others have written children's books on Jesus and the fishermen of the Sea of Galilee, and Mary Robb Wilson wrote *Soulshine* on that subject. The books are commercially available.

Appreciations

I express particular appreciation to Rev. Mark S. Anschutz, Carol Ann Bernheim, Jane Cocke Black, Amb. J. Kenneth and Rosa Blackwell, Fr. Edward Cappelletti, SDB, Fr. James Chiosso, SDB, Rev. Wade Hampton Dean, Dr. Donald J. Devine, Fr. Augustyn Dziedziel, SDB, Stanislaw Cardinal Dziwisz, Bruce Eberle, Dr. W. Lee Edwards and Elizabeth Edwards Spalding, Edmund Tazewell Ellett, Timothy S, Goeglein, Fr. William L. George, SJ, Theodossis Georgiou and Dr. Aliki Mitsakos, Stephen Humphrey, Karen T. Huntley, Fred and Lesley Israel, June Alice Leonard, Ferdinand Mahfood, M. Peter and Joanne McPherson, Kelsey Merritt, Dr. Eric Patterson, Roger R. Ream, Alfred S. Regnery, Bertha Mae Rippey Rhew, Rabbi David Rosen, Mary Kathleen King Rothschild, Arnold Steinberg, Darlene McKinnon Teague, Jessica Townsend Teague, Cornell Townsend and James Teague and Mary Robb Teague Wilson, Michael W. and Katherine B. Thompson and Michael W. Thompson, Jr., H. Stetson Tinkham, Lexi Vanatta, Brian and Anne Waidmann, W. Bruce Weinrod, Geneva Welch, Michael L. Wilson, Dr. Jose Antonio Zaglul, and Anthony Ziccardi.

Their value to me ranged from inspiring me to address the centrality in our lives of religious teachings and lives seeking to reflect them, through encouraging me to undertake this inquiry and its reduction to a writing, sometimes without them even being aware of that encouragement, to assistance in navigating research, reducing premises and conclusions to words, and to achieving a coherent manuscript for publication.

The words in these pages are solely mine. I take responsibility for them and absolve each of any responsibility for them as expressed by me. If I failed to recall others by name for their giving of time and talent in bringing this book to publication, I offer my apologies. Remind me, and I will add them to any second edition.

I express my appreciation also to authors, researchers, and others, associations and organizations, and the words and images set forth above, whose aspirations, inspirations, memberships, publications, and websites enabled this work to move from an idea, through research and writing, to past, present, and, I hope, future bookshelves, Kindles, and equivalents. They are set out above because they were of informational, educational, and sometimes inspirational value, but none of them has endorsed in any manner whatsoever what I have set out, especially because they have not even known of this text.

I did not footnote or endnote statements made in these pages for two reasons. Though its subject matters are history, religion, and philosophy found through the lives and legacies of several fishermen and their Master, I offer it to its readers as a memoir of my own spiritual journey in their footsteps. Furthermore, by not making specific references to statements written, it encourages readers to explore on their own, rather than follow noted explorations, and to be informed and encouraged by their own findings.

About the Author

Photo by Kristen Underwood

Believing in the value of St. Augustine's "The world is a book, and he who stays at home reads only one page," Randal Teague has studied human behavior and its ties to faith in over one hundred countries.

Born in Durham and raised in Chapel Hill, North Carolina and along Florida's Gulf Coast, he first imagined a future in marine biology before finding another in law and charitable activities. That latter path drew him to our nation's capital where he completed college and law school and fostered a lifelong commitment to individual liberty, democratic institutions, and international development.

Teague earned three degrees and received two in honors from universities in the United States and overseas. His children call him the "Energizer Bunny" for he seldom rests.